HORIZON

MARCH, 1960 · VOLUME II, NUMBER 4

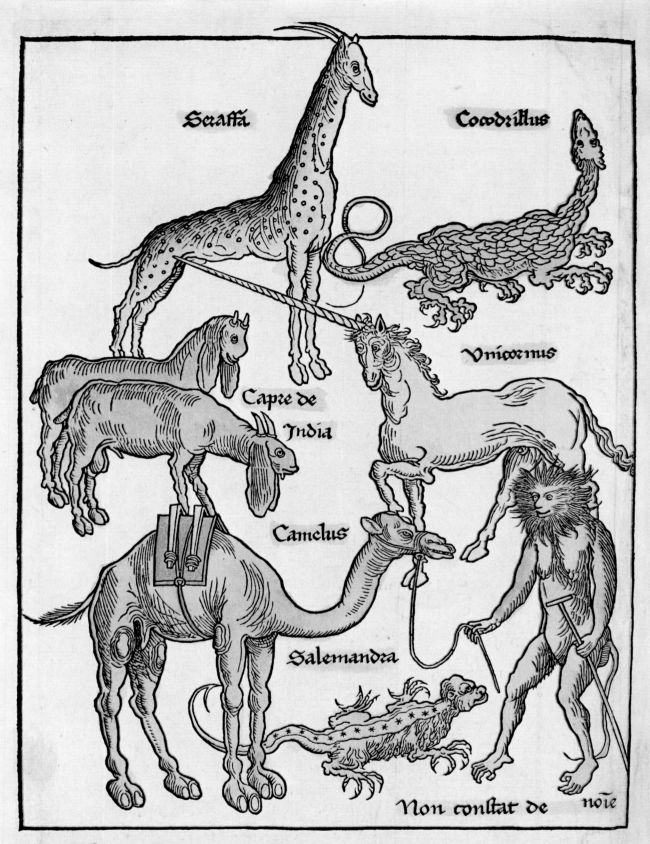

Seraffa   Cocodrillus

Capre de Jndia   Vnicornus

Camelus

Salemandra

Non conſtat de   noīe

Hec animalia ſunt veraciter depicta ſicut vidimus in terra ſancta

HORIZON

A Magazine of the Arts

MARCH, 1960 · VOLUME II, NUMBER 4

PUBLISHER
James Parton

EDITOR
Joseph J. Thorndike, Jr.

MANAGING EDITOR
William Harlan Hale

ASSOCIATE EDITORS
Ralph Backlund
Robert Emmett Ginna

ASSISTANT EDITORS
Ada Pesin
Jane Wilson

EDITORIAL ASSISTANTS
Shirley Abbott, Caroline Backlund,
Alan Doré, Martha Thomson

COPY EDITOR
Mary Ann Pfeiffer
Assistants: Rebecca R. Barocas, Ruth Limmer

ART DIRECTOR
Irwin Glusker
Assistant: Emma Landau

ADVISORY BOARD
Gilbert Highet, *Chairman*
Frederick Burkhardt   Oliver Jensen
Marshall B. Davidson   Jotham Johnson
Richard M. Ketchum

EUROPEAN CONSULTING EDITOR
J. H. Plumb
Christ's College, Cambridge

EUROPEAN BUREAU
Gertrudis Feliu, *Chief*
28 Quai du Louvre, Paris

CIRCULATION DIRECTOR
Richard V. Benson

HORIZON is published every two months by
American Horizon, Inc., a subsidiary of American
Heritage Publishing Co., Inc., 551 Fifth Avenue,
New York 17, N. Y.
      Single Copies: $3.95
Annual Subscriptions: $18.00 in the U.S. & Can.
                   $19.00 elsewhere

Second-Class postage paid at New York, N.Y.

HORIZON welcomes contributions but can assume
no responsibility for such unsolicited material.

COVER: This pair of lovers caught in the act of fleeing, with drapery flying, from a sudden squall form the central images of the huge painting, *The Storm*, by Pierre Auguste Cot, reproduced in its entirety on page 60. Painted in 1880 for the French Salon trade, it has belonged to the Metropolitan Museum of Art since 1887. Although most of the once fashionable academic paintings of the nineteenth century remaining in museum collections have long since been relegated to basement storage, Cot's "classical" tour de force occupies a place on a gallery wall. An article about Salon paintings both in their prime and decline begins on page 52.

FRONTISPIECE: Arrayed beside the more prosaic goats and camel in this fifteenth-century woodcut are such zoological marvels as a long-horned giraffe, a unicorn, a star-spangled salamander, and a near relative of the Abominable Snowman. Although the artist hedges a bit on the latter ("There is no agreement about the name" the Latin caption reads), he flatly asserts: "These animals are truthfully depicted just as we saw them in the Holy Land." This is an illustration from Breydenbach's *Travels in the Holy Land,* published in Mainz in 1486. An article about another pilgrim who made the same journey begins on page 81.

WHAT GOOD IS TELEVISION

Mostly it has been a funnel for things that stage or screen do better. But in forms like the visual essay it discovers its own nature. A critic warns the spoiled baby of the art forms to quit playing with borrowed gold and make its own creative way

For twenty-five years or more everyone kept explaining that the art of the motion picture was still in its infancy; then suddenly, almost without warning, it seemed to be dying of old age. Television is in its infancy now; I wonder if a premature senility is just around the corner.

I am not in the least concerned, in these remarks, with the youthful indiscretions that human concupiscence is always ready to visit upon any art that is also an industry: quiz scandals, poor programing for children, that sort of thing. Any medium can ride out an incident of corruption. What it cannot ride out is a corruption of form.

Forms concern me. The birth, maturity, and death of any entertainment medium is a fascinating, sometimes exhilarating, and sometimes saddening process to follow. And we must all of us face the fact that forms do not necessarily find themselves. No natural law protects a Johnny-come-lately in the arts, guaranteeing it a period of ripe maturity before it breathes its last. It is possible for one or another kind of promised delight to lose its way before it has quite learned to walk, for it to walk thereafter in the wilderness with a limp, and to grow old without ever having grown straight.

Let me explain. I do some work in television, and I am fortunate to be able to do it in the company of some of the most intelligent and creative people I know. Last spring I was part of a project that most of the newspapers found adventurous and farseeing: the recording on magnetic tape of a program staged entirely "on location." Until that time most taping had been done in studios, under pleasantly controlled conditions. But the scenery, the caves and bridges for such an extravaganza as *For Whom the Bell Tolls*, had looked like studio scenery, and the venture I was associated with—an hour-long dramatization of H. L. Tredree's *The*

By WALTER KERR

Strange Ordeal of the Normandier—was about to try for something else: for an on-the-spot atmosphere that would remove all traces of hothouse fabrication. Tredree's factual narrative had to do with a maritime disaster of World War One: the harrowing days of a British tramp ship pressed into service without adequate equipment and left powerless to drift through hurricanes while most of her crew died of fever. It was decided to move cast and cables over to Bayonne, New Jersey, where an old destroyer was used for a stage and where fire-boats poured tons of water over listing actors to produce a highly believable simulation of hurricane seas.

After three days of work the tape was completed, and on the following Sunday afternoon I was able to watch it in my living room. It had flaws: the splicing of pieces of tape is a new and difficult technique, and wherever splicing had been necessary the image "rolled over" on the television screen; some sequences seemed to have been shot through dirty wire mesh; the louder the gale, the less intelligible were the Cockney accents. It had virtues: authenticity, spectacle, speed in the making, and speed in the viewing.

The newspaper notices, as I have said, were generally admiring. The telephone calls that flowed in after the program were congratulatory. And I was still in shock.

What I had watched on Sunday afternoon was not a television show at all. It was a 1933 British movie.

My relief that so vulnerable a project had not ended in patent disaster kept me from arguing too heatedly with the television professionals I met during the next few days. When I did express doubt about the quality of the program, it was generally assumed that I was being prematurely captious about the mechanics of tape. In time, I was assured, the shaky photography would grow firm, the sound would spruce up, and the splicing would glide by with the grace of the river Clitumnus.

There can be no doubt that these assurances are valid. If the program I had seen had been recorded three years from now, instead of at the dawn of a new method, it would certainly have been clean, supple, and superbly convincing. It would then have looked like a 1963 British movie.

But is there anything really wrong with a television show's looking like a British movie, or an American movie, or a movie of any kind? I think there may be. There is, first of all, a practical problem: a form is straining every nerve to compete where it cannot compete. The most generous of television budgets, after all, demands that a tape recording be completed in three to four weeks at most. And a program assembled under these conditions, barring that odd act of genius on which no one can count, is probably not going to duplicate the quality John Huston will achieve, given six to nine months and three to five million dollars, filming the same materials off the west coast of Africa. The practical problem is not half so important as a problem that pops up the minute the practical one is solved. Suppose the unlikely happens, that the accident of genius intervenes, and the com-

pleted entertainment succeeds in competing with its wealthier and more experienced rival—what then? Television will have turned into its rival. It will have ceased being itself.

Of course, television may be without a self to worry about.

It is conceivable that television is not a form at all, but simply a convenient device for channeling other forms into millions of homes. In this case, it is no more than an impersonal instrument, like an artificial hearing-aid or a pair of bifocals. Its live shows are stage shows, dramatic or musical, faithfully transmitted. Its films are films, somewhat reduced in size. Its tapes are films of a quick-mix kind, photographs developed in the camera without a side trip to the laboratory. If these things are so, there is no reason under heaven why the medium should not appropriate every gadget that is available to it, refine each gadget until it purrs, and content itself with marketing all things to all men and no one particular thing to anybody.

If I am not wholly convinced that television is an anonymous delivery boy incapable of a creative act of its own—a funnel without a face—it is because I have, on one occasion or another, seen something happen on the home screen that could not, within reason, have happened anywhere else. It is an accident of time and place that I stumbled upon the first of Agnes de Mille's essays on choreography for *Omnibus* before I had ever seen a Leonard Bernstein seminar in music: Mr. Bernstein is the man who shaped the curious combination of intimate discussion and massive illustration that has so handsomely served a few of his contemporaries. Watching the De Mille show, I was thunderstruck—not so much by the quality of the program, which was superb, but by my own realization that there was nowhere else in the world I could go to find this.

Though it was something of a lecture, I could not look for it in a classroom: there is no classroom that could accommodate, or afford, the scale of the illustration. Though hers might have been called a concert-with-comment (Mr. Bernstein is now arriving at just such a mixture in his "preview" evenings at Carnegie Hall), I could not hope to find my experience duplicated, in just this way, in an auditorium. Here I had a mobile camera to reach out for, and stress, accents. Though the mobile camera was essential to its uniqueness, I could never expect to see its like in a motion-picture theater: the motion-picture theater, like the legitimate playhouse, is essentially and properly devoted to narrative. What I was watching, I told myself, was an entirely new form: the visual essay. And because television had managed to arrange its resources in such a way that no rival medium could claim, or even aspire, to offer precisely the same experience, television had, for me, acquired an identity.

Thereafter, I knew what sort of program I could not afford to miss. I could miss the westerns and catch them at Loew's. I could miss the dramas and see better on Broadway. I could skip the news analysts and read Walter Lippmann.

CONTINUED ON PAGE 126

FROM THE CLASSIC EARTH

Last year two laborers were repairing a sewer in Piraeus, the seaport of Athens, when they stumbled on a hoard of masterpieces of Greek sculpture lost since antiquity and lying barely a yard beneath the pavement. Of the eight works found, the marvels are four bronze statues, which Horizon was enabled to photograph through the courtesy of Ionnis Papadimitriou, Director of Antiquities for the Greek government. They are presented here virtually as they came from the earth, with fissures, marks of corrosion, and particles of soil still on them.

First, opposite, is the upper portion of a figure of the goddess Artemis, standing five feet high. A Hellenistic work of the fourth century B.C., its warm grace and air of thoughtful quiet exemplify the finest qualities of that sculptural period. Unquestionably the greatest of the finds is the magnificent *kouros*, or youth, shown overleaf—probably a representation of the god Apollo. Made in the late sixth century B.C., this slightly more than life-size figure is the earliest statue in bronze that has yet come to light from the soil of Greece. While it still conveys the stylized simplicity of the archaic, its forms reveal the gentle swell of life and the naturalness that characterize the art of the classic period.

On the left-hand page thereafter appears the larger than life-size head of a girl, her eyes set with semi-precious stones and fixed in a serene gaze. Close to the school of Praxiteles, the whole statue sums up what was best in Greek art near the close of the fourth century B.C. The final page presents a figure of Athena in her splendor. More than seven feet high, it is a triumph of a sculptor active near the beginning of the fourth century. The goddess is heroic and magisterial in her great helmet, adorned with shapes of owls and griffons. Across her breast is fitted the *aegis*, in its center the head of Medusa with its hair of serpents.

Some evidence on the site has led scholars to theorize that the works may have been brought together at Piraeus as part of a shipment of artistic loot destined for Rome, and that the warehouse containing them may have burned during the pillaging of Athens and Piraeus by the troops of the dictator Sulla in 86 B.C. Whatever the circumstances, at some ancient moment they were buried and forgotten, and their cover of oblivion perfectly preserved them from further marauders for the gaze of our own time.

PHOTOGRAPHS BY D. A. HARISSIADIS, ATHENS

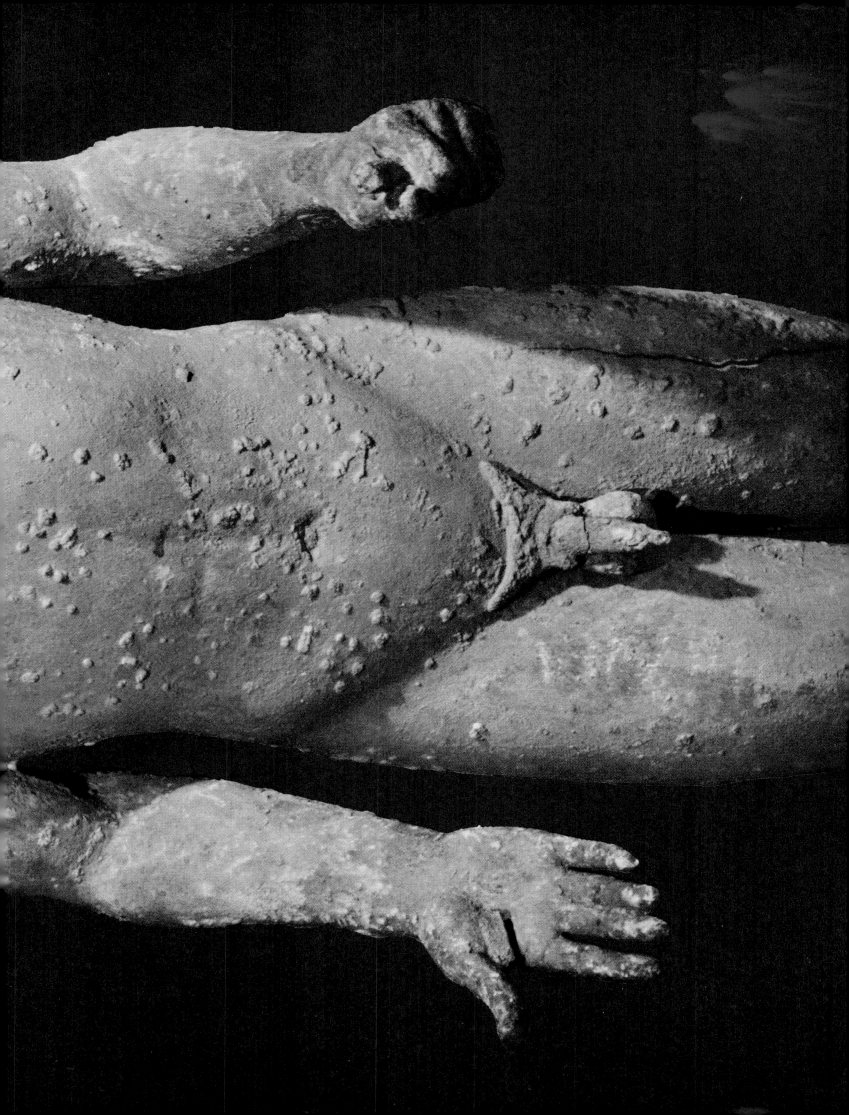

MAN'S WAY WITH THE WILDERNESS

He has by turns feared it, disdained it, reveled in it,

and despoiled it. His arts reflect his varying attitudes

to it. Today he is learning to prize what is left of it

By PAUL BROOKS

Although my subject is as broad as all outdoors, I can define its limits without going far afield. Take, at one pole, the rejoinder of the famous Boston wit and scholar Helen Bell, to a friend who innocently remarked on a beautiful spring morning that she was going for a walk in the country. "Well," said Mrs. Bell sourly, "kick a tree for me."

Take at the other pole Henry David Thoreau, who despised cities and believed that "in wildness is the preservation of the world." Somebody said of Thoreau that he could get more out of ten minutes with a woodchuck than most men could get from a night with Cleopatra. These are the extremes. In any place and in any period there is obviously an infinite variety of individual attitudes toward nature, all the way from the gushing "Oh-the-wonder-of-it" approach of sentimental "nature-writers" to the laconic Englishman whose only comment on being shown the great fall of water at Niagara was: "What's to stop it?"

Leaving personal idiosyncrasies aside, it is possible to trace in broad outline the changing pattern of man's relationship to wild nature throughout history. Nor is this merely an academic exercise. Only within our lifetime have technology and population pressure reached the point where absolute control—or more accurately, absolute destruction—of the world's remaining wilderness becomes a real possibility. Our attitude toward nature is therefore a matter of immediate concern. What is that attitude, and where did it come from?

Our Western cultural tradition, particularly in its Old Testament origins, has a wholly different concept of nature from that of the East. To the Hindu, all nature is to some extent divine, and is valued for its own sake; there is an intimate relation between man and the rest of creation. The Chinese artist who, after years of study and contemplation, paints a shaft of bamboo swaying in the wind *is*, for the instant, that bamboo feeling the wind in its leaves; when he paints a landscape he is lost among its mountains; human figures or the works of man are purely incidental.

Though the Old Testament—in the Psalms, in Job, in Isaiah—is full of appreciation and awe of the natural world,

Opposite: A medieval sense of the wilderness as a menacing presence is conveyed in Albrecht Altdorfer's Forest Landscape with St. George, *painted in 1511 (detail at far left), while in thirteenth-century China, Ts'ao Chih-Pai depicts man as being blissfully at one with surrounding nature.*

this world was first and foremost a garment of the Lord, significant in relation to the Creator who was above it all. ("The heavens declare the glory of God; and the firmament sheweth his handywork.") Man was created in God's image; and the rest of the world was made to be dominated and used by man: "Be fruitful, and multiply, and replenish the earth, and *subdue* it: and have dominion over the fish of the sea, and over the fowl of the air, and over every living thing that moveth upon the earth." From here it was only a short step to the philosophy that whatever was not "useful" was somehow vicious, and to the idea still prevalent today that the natural world is merely a commodity to be exploited. Whereas the Chinese had a religious fervor for wild places, to the primitive Western mind they were wastelands inhabited by evil spirits.

In comparing the Eastern and the Western painters' approach to landscape, Benjamin Rowland points out that whereas in Greece a dryad, or wood nymph, *personified* a grove or a tree, in China and Japan the grove or tree itself was divine. In the Middle Ages, these Greek gods became demons to plague holy men in the woods, as robbers plagued early travelers. "For more than a thousand years," says Rowland, "the wilderness became a kind of symbol of the sinful and unholy. . . . It was only in the seventeenth century, when the demons and the dangers were cleared out from the underbrush, that there began a serious and philosophic speculation about nature and a poetic and artistic interpretation of her moods."

Returning to the Greeks, we find in Homer an abundance of similes from wild nature, though Ruskin claims that "every Homeric landscape, intended to be beautiful, is composed of a fountain, a meadow, and a shady grove . . . Homer, living in mountainous and rocky countries, dwells delightedly on all the flat bits." The Romans, like the Greeks before them, had a greater love for gentle and orderly landscape than they had for wild areas and craggy peaks. Lucretius says that mountains are to be avoided, and Cicero grudgingly remarks that any place where you happen to live eventually becomes pleasing, "even though it be a mountain or a forest."

During the Middle Ages, the most impressive building sites from the point of view of wild mountain scenery were occupied by the Church: Monte Cassino, Chamonix, La Grand Chartreuse, and so on. Besides being cheap—since no one else wanted them—and easily defended, many such sites already had religious associations and undoubtedly encouraged the contemplative life. Certainly there is a connection between the religious temperament and identification with the wild. But it must have been difficult for a man of the Middle Ages, monk or layman, to have a deep appreciation of the spiritual value of the material world around him if he believed that it was only a sort of Ellis Island on the threshold of the Heavenly Kingdom.

With the coming of the Renaissance and the increasing concern for things of the present world as against those of the next, this attitude began slowly to change. As Havelock Ellis has pointed out, the Renaissance movement toward nature was a revival, in more elaborate and more intense form, of the enjoyment of nature in classical times. It was not primarily an attraction toward wild nature, "but it embraced elements of the love of the wild, and these were notably shown in a new and actively adventurous love of mountains." Dante was apparently a mountain climber. But it is Petrarch who provides the perfect example of the change in point of view, and why it came so hard. In a letter describing an ascent of Mt. Ventoux near Avignon, he tells how he was charmed and uplifted by the magnificent views from the summit. Then, unfortunately, "it occurred to me to take out the copy of St. Augustine's Confessions that I always kept with me. . . . And I call God to witness that the first words on which I cast my eyes were these: 'Men go to wonder at the heights of mountains, the ocean floods, rivers' long courses, ocean's immensity, the revolutions of the stars —and of themselves they have no care!' . . . I closed the book, angry with myself for not ceasing to admire things of earth, instead of remembering that the human soul is beyond comparison the subject for admiration."

Meanwhile, in England, the poets—always the most sensitive indicators of the spirits of the time—had begun to write about nature with that loving intimacy which has always been so much a part of English life and literature. Chaucer's love of nature, with its special celebration of spring, is fresh and immediate rather than literary, though it is confined to the comparatively tame countryside of Surrey and Kent. Shakespeare's plays and sonnets are, of course, full of superb nature imagery based on a countryman's (not to mention a deer poacher's) intimate acquaintance with the outdoors. It has been remarked how much of the action in the plays is carried out under the open sky. Only the grandeur of mountains was outside his experience.

Alas, in literature as well as in life, "summer's lease hath all too short a date." In the century following Shakespeare's death—the century in which the American colonies were being founded—"the darling buds of May" were transformed into wax flowers under glass. Wilderness became distasteful. Nature was tolerated only where it was regimented and housebroken; it was a servant or it was an enemy. Milton could get along very well without "Mountains on whose barren breast/ The labouring clouds do often rest." Even

Andrew Marvell, who wrote almost ecstatically of gardens, and who enjoyed green thoughts in a green shade, could describe mountains as "ill-designed excrescences that deform the earth and frighten heaven." To Alexander Pope, the moon is the "refulgent lamp of night," and shepherds going about their business are "conscious swains" who "bless the useful light." One is reminded of *The New Yorker* cartoon by Helen Hokinson of a lady, dressing for dinner, who asks the maid, "Margaret, is there a moon?"

The passion for order and regimentation reaches a climax in Burnet's *Theory of the Earth*, in which he expresses regret that the stars had not been more artistically arranged:

They lie carelessly scatter'd, as if they had been sown in the Heaven, like Seed, by handfuls; and not by a skilful hand neither. What a beautiful Hemisphere they would have made, if they had been plac'd in rank and order, if they had been all dispos'd into regular figures, and the little ones set with due regard to the greater. Then all finisht and made up into one fair piece or great Composition, according to the rules of Art and Symmetry.

You can't go much further than that.

Meanwhile, in France, Jean Jacques Rousseau was starting a revolution in man's attitude toward nature. In contrast to Mme de Staël, who is said to have drawn the curtains of her carriage as she passed the Alps, Rousseau preached the gospel of nature in ecstatic terms, rhapsodizing and swooning at everything outdoors—sunrise, breezes, flowers, birds, trees, torrents, precipices. Though this ceaseless rapture becomes rather cloying, and though he had a streak of morbid sentimentality, Rousseau certainly performed an immense service in breaking the old patterns of thought, in bringing about a new sensibility and awareness of the out-of-doors. His rapturous view of nature found its finest expression in the English poets of the romantic revival: Wordsworth's "Prelude" and "Tintern Abbey," and Shelley's "Mont Blanc" are inspired by a sense of identification with the rest of nature, a willingness to value it for its own sake, on its own terms, which is not unlike that of the Chinese.

Meanwhile, what of the Englishmen who had crossed the Atlantic and really knew the wilderness, on a grand and terrifying scale, at first hand? To the early settlers the virgin forest was anything but romantic. It was an enemy to be conquered. And that is natural enough. If you have ever tramped hour after hour through one of our remaining fragments of primeval forest, where the ground is a tangle of roots and the sun barely penetrates through the dense green canopy, you will understand what the frontiersman was up against in clearing an open patch for a stand of corn. And in New England, even if he were able to appreciate the grandeur as well as the challenge of his environment, his puritan training—his suspicion of beauty divorced from utility—would put a damper on any such delights. To Michael

Wigglesworth, writing in 1662, everything beyond the cleared area of the settlements was

A waste and howling wilderness,
Where none inhabited
But hellish fiends, and brutish men
That Devils worshipped.

Yet there were exceptions. Jonathan Edwards had a deep appreciation of wild solitudes and rugged natural beauty, which he reconciled with his religion by considering all worldly splendors to be mere shadows of the awful majesty of God. And there is a magnificent passage from Samuel Sewall which suggests that even the Puritans felt in their bones that man's salvation lay in his fellowship with nature, rather than in his dominion over it. Judge Sewall, in the very year that he stood before the congregation of the Old South Church to confess his error in condemning the Salem witches, published an esoteric theological tract about the world to come. In the midst of it his mind strayed to the beloved Plum Island of his boyhood:

As long as *Plum Island* shall faithfully keep the commanded Post; Notwithstanding all the hectoring Words, and hard Blows of the proud and boisterous Ocean; As long as any Salmon, or Sturgeon shall swim in the streams of *Merrimack*; or any Perch, or Pickeril, in *Crane Pond;* As long as the Sea-Fowl shall know the Time of their coming, and not neglect seasonably to visit the Places of their Acquaintance; As long as any Cattel shall be fed with the Grass growing in the Medows, which do humbly bow down themselves before *Turkie-Hill*; As long as any Sheep shall walk upon *Old Town Hills,* and shall from thence pleasantly look down upon the *River Parker,* and the fruitful Marishes lying beneath; As long as any free & harmless Doves shall find a White Oak, or other Tree within the Township, to perch, or feed, or build a careless Nest upon; and shall voluntarily present themselves to perform the office of Gleaners after Barley-Harvest; As long as Nature shall not grow Old and dote; but shall constantly remember to give the rows of Indian Corn their education, by Pairs: So long shall Christians be born there; and being first made meet shall from thence be Translated, to be made partakers of the Inheritance of the Saints in Light.

This is a far cry from the Wigglesworth of a generation earlier. Of course the frontier was rapidly retreating. By the time of the Revolution a good deal of the howling wilderness had been subdued with fire and ax; and the hellish fiends, who had proved no match for the "saints in light," were about to be reborn at a safe distance as noble savages. There was also growing up a scientific as well as an aesthetic interest in a flora and fauna that was wholly new to the naturalists of Europe.

Benjamin Franklin was interested in nature as he was in everything else. His approach was practical rather than aesthetic. He encouraged conservation, and surely approved a paper read by a member of the Philosophical Society in 1789, which was concerned with more than timber values: "Our stately forests are a natural treasure, deserving the solicitious care of the patriotic philosopher and politician."

True understanding of wild nature was to be found not so much among the literary people as among the naturalist-explorers, who knew what they were talking about and were writers only incidentally. The most famous of these were the great ornithologist Alexander Wilson and John James Audubon. However, there was one professional writer, an almost exact contemporary of Audubon, who found his greatest inspiration in the American forest. It is somehow fitting that James Fenimore Cooper's most popular book, *The Last of the Mohicans,* and Audubon's most popular print of the American wild turkey should both have been born in 1826. Both men were romantics, both preferred wild America to the studied beauties of Europe, and both resented the senseless waste of its treasures. Leatherstocking sees something almost impious in the cutting of the forests, the seining of the rivers, the slaughter of the passenger pigeons.

But the first American wholly committed to the values of wild nature was Henry Thoreau. He was, I think, more of a poet and a prophet than a naturalist. He was a prophet crying *for* the wilderness. He felt that there were enough champions of civilization. He wanted to speak for "absolute freedom and wildness . . . to regard man as an inhabitant, and a part and parcel of Nature." He identified himself with nature as completely perhaps as the Oriental philosophers whom he delighted to read. He felt wiser in all respects for knowing that there was a minnow in the brook: "Methinks I have need even of his sympathy, and to be his fellow in a degree." In his journal he tells how he watched from far off the felling of one of the last great pines on Fairhaven Hill. He might be describing the assassination of a king.

Thoreau said that when he went out for a walk with no particular objective in mind, his inner compass always settled between west and south-southwest. The west to him was "but another name for the Wild." Of course he saw the Far West only in his imagination. Its prophet was to be a man in some ways like Thoreau, in others very different.

John Muir also rejected the idea that the world was made especially for man. "Whole kingdoms of creatures enjoyed existence and returned to dust ere man appeared to claim them. After human beings have also played their part in Creation's plan, they too may disappear without any general burning or extraordinary commotion whatever." Yet men "are painfully astonished whenever they find anything, living or dead, in all God's universe, which they cannot eat or render in some way what they call useful to themselves."

Muir, however, was neither the philosopher nor the mystic that Thoreau was. He could find God in a water ouzel, but he could never have gone round the world by the Old Marlborough Road. When Muir talks about wilderness he means wilderness on the grand scale—giant redwoods and the High Sierra, not a blueberry patch and a swamp along the Concord River. He was dedicated to an idea, but he was also canny and practical: he could get on with people as well as with woodchucks. It is well that he could. The time had come to back up philosophical speculation with political action. In

Europe the virgin wilderness had disappeared little by little, virtually unnoticed. In America, perhaps because of the dramatic speed with which we raped the land, a cry arose at last to save something of what was left. And owing to our political tradition, it was to be saved not in the form of huge private estates or hunting preserves, but as national parks for the enjoyment of all the people.

On June 25, 1864, while General Sherman was preparing to destroy as much of Georgia as possible, President Lincoln signed a Congressional bill to save from commercial exploitation Yosemite Valley and its giant sequoias. Frederick Law Olmsted, the great proponent of the park idea, administered the area under the aegis of the state of California, until he went East to superintend the construction of Central Park in New York City. Though it began as a state park, Yosemite set the precedent when Yellowstone National Park was established a few years later. Here was the beginning of the national park system. It is the first example in recorded history of sustained effort on the part of any people to preserve native landscape for its own sake—an example which has since been followed throughout the world.

At first the emphasis was on the preservation of geological wonders. Later came the protection—sometimes misguided —of flora and fauna. Last of all has arisen the idea that certain parts of the national forests and parks, as yet untouched, should be preserved for all time as "wilderness areas"—free from lumbering or other exploitation, roadless, accessible only by trail or canoe. This is a relatively new concept, at least in terms of political action, and is taking hold none too soon. Less than 2½ per cent of our land can still be properly described as "wilderness," almost all of it in the West, and under Federal ownership or control. There are forty-eight areas so classified in our national parks, eighty-two in our national forests (constituting only 8 per cent of total national forest area). Even this remnant is threatened by multiple forms of exploitation: by highways and power dams, by lumber and mining interests, by "recreational" developments and commercial pressures of every kind. Our government has never had an over-all national policy for the preservation of its wilderness as such. Now at last we have such a policy and program in the "Wilderness Bill," recently introduced in Congress after years of research and effort on the part of devoted individuals and conservation groups.

The wilderness program gives political expression to man's instinctive need—as Joseph Wood Krutch expresses it—to experience a world we did not make. "Wilderness and the idea of wilderness," writes Krutch, "is one of the permanent homes of the human spirit." Edwin Way Teale puts it a slightly different way: "Going to the wilderness is not a flight from life. It is escape—but escape to reality, escape from all that is artificial in civilization."

Today the clearest voices raised in support of wilderness values come not from the ivory tower, but from men and women who have followed the forest trails, plumbed the canyons, traversed the portages, sought the treasure of the tidepools at the edge of the sea.

Civilized man no longer fears wild nature: there is not much left of it to fear. Today Mrs. Bell's friend who was going for a walk in the country would be going for a drive in suburbia, and she might be hard put to it to find a tree worth kicking. If we have given up the idea of arranging the stars in straight lines, we are rearranging the balance of nature on earth to an extent that may eventually topple the whole structure. Modern science, of course, has made this possible, but modern science has also demonstrated what the poets and prophets have intuitively felt all along—man's essential kinship with the rest of nature. As Professor Paul B. Sears of Yale says: "Morality today involves a responsible relationship toward the laws of the natural world of which we are inescapably a part. Violence toward nature, as the Tao has it, is no less evil than violence toward fellow-man."

Paul Brooks, chief editor of the Houghton Mifflin Company, often travels in and writes about the American wilderness.

AN AMERICA
STILL UNTAMED BY MAN

A Portfolio by Ansel Adams

Few artists in our time have identified themselves so intimately with their chosen subject as Ansel Adams, whose photographs of still untouched natural fastnesses within the United States appear on the following eight pages. Born in San Francisco in 1902 and first trained as a concert pianist, he gave up a musical career at twenty-eight to pursue the twin lures of the camera and the wilderness. A naturalist and ardent conservationist, he has traveled widely in the roughest regions of the continent beyond the reach of roads or familiar trails, has lived in the Yosemite preserve, and emerges from the wilds fired chiefly with a desire to return into them. An innovator in photographic technique, he is most notable for the poetic angle of vision he brings to bear on crag and desert, on great and little waters alike. In fully twenty books and portfolios, Adams has recorded various steps of his personal immersion in the dwindling American wilderness he prizes and defends.

On the following pages:
1 Virgin undergrowth in Mount Rainier National Park
2 Snake River and the Grand Teton Range, Wyoming
3 The Oregon coast, south from Cape Sebastian
4 Mount McKinley, Alaska, seen from a high pass
5 Sand dunes, Death Valley, southern California

START
of a
LONG DAY'S JOURNEY

The New London Youth of Eugene O'Neill

At his death in 1953, Eugene O'Neill was not only America's greatest dramatist, but he had achieved a pre-eminent position among the playwrights of the world in this century. He had thrice won a Pulitzer prize, in 1920, 1922, and 1928, as well as a Nobel prize in 1936. Posthumously, he received a Pulitzer prize for *Long Day's Journey into Night* in 1957. His plays, translated into many languages, may well be read and viewed today by more people than the work of any other playwright except Shakespeare.

Since his death, O'Neill's troubled and sometimes lurid life has attracted the attention of several biographers. But the definitive biography is likely to be that by Arthur and Barbara Gelb, which will be published by Harper and Brothers late next fall under the title *The Life of Eugene O'Neill.*

Mr. Gelb, a theater reporter and critic for *The New York Times,* and his wife, a free-lance writer, corresponded with or interviewed some eight hundred persons in their quest. They gained access to many documents heretofore closely guarded by O'Neill and others who had shared his torments. On the following fifteen pages, HORIZON presents sections from two chapters of the Gelbs' book dealing with the least known years of O'Neill's life, his youth in New London.

The playwright was to return to this period for much of his material. In the dedication to his last masterpiece, *Long Day's Journey into Night,* O'Neill tacitly acknowledged that the play was drawn from the circumstances of his own family in New London, and that in writing it he had performed both an act of love and expiation for the bitterness that had raged in his heart since the days of his youth. In these chapters, the Gelbs create a minutely rendered picture of a time, a place, the persons and events against which we may observe the growth of an artist.

The playwright once remarked that he was concerned essentially with the relationship between man and God. This concern informs his tragedies, which present a view of a world in which idealists are destroyed by the frailty of their own mortal being. Like Joyce, a writer to whom he is related by more than race, O'Neill could never escape his youth. In it he formed the tragic view that was to account for his greatness and his haunted days.

Eugene O'Neill as he appeared in 1913. Twenty-five years old and just out of a sanatorium, he was beginning his career as a dramatist.

The New London Youth of Eugene O'Neill

The town of New London, Connecticut, was the closest thing to a home that Eugene O'Neill knew as a boy. After being dragged about the country as a very young child by his celebrated actor-father, James O'Neill, Eugene spent the years between his seventh and seventeenth birthday at Catholic boarding schools and a fashionable boarding-preparatory school. His father, whose fame and success were always far greater on the road than on Broadway, returned every summer to New London, there to play at being the head of a cozily established and united family. But in fact the O'Neills were nothing of the kind. In addition to Eugene and James, the family consisted of James's neurotic, withdrawn wife, Ella—periodically the victim of a narcotics addiction originating at Eugene's birth—and their disappointing, dissolute older son, Jamie. Ella accompanied James on his tours, and the O'Neills' summer reunions with their children were invariably marked by disharmony. Although they all loved each other fiercely, they could not communicate their love, and the pride of each caused constant friction.

New London, at the time James O'Neill bought a home there in the mid-1880's, was one of the most beautiful towns in the East. Built on a succession of low hills, it boasted a large, deep-water harbor—a continuation of the Thames River that leads out into Long Island Sound—which made a magnificent natural anchorage for ships of any size, including the square-riggers, colorful Sound steamers, and windjammers that still sailed the seas.

The town's mainstay in the 1880's was small industry, revolving around shipping, textiles, and the tag end of the whaling business, but its possibilities as a summer resort were already being recognized. A sprinkling of the socially prominent from such cities as New York, Boston, Philadelphia, and New Orleans, acknowledging New London as a yachting and swimming paradise, were beginning to build huge summer homes on the long avenue later called Pequot, which ran alongside the Thames to its mouth. Within a dozen years New London had become an elegant resort town, rivaling Newport and Narragansett Pier for its accumulation of wealthy vacationers,

and it was in this atmosphere that young O'Neill spent his summers.

Those summer months in New London with his family made an indelible impression on O'Neill. He was to set three of his major plays there—Ah, Wilderness!, Long Day's Journey into Night, and A Moon for the Misbegotten —and parts of many others.

In the fall of 1932, Eugene O'Neill wrote his only full-length comedy. He called it *Ah, Wilderness!*, set it in a "large-small town in Connecticut" in the summer of 1906, and made its central character, Richard Miller, a boy "going on seventeen, just out of high school" and ready to enter Yale in the fall. Eugene, who was seventeen, just out of high school and ready to enter Princeton in the fall, spent the summer of 1906 in the large-small town of New London.

When *Ah, Wilderness!* was produced, there was a great deal of speculation as to how autobiographical the characters and events of the play had been. Its author said at the time that the resemblance between the circumstances of Richard Miller's life and his own were

By ARTHUR *and* BARBARA GELB

trifling, except in a few minor details. What he actually thought of himself and his family did not emerge until *Long Day's Journey into Night,* set in the New London of 1912, made its appearance twenty-four years later. *Ah, Wilderness!,* said O'Neill, was a nostalgic dream of what he would have liked his adolescence to be. "The truth is, I *had* no youth," he added.

His nostalgia about the summer of 1906, when O'Neill was between school and college—a period of significance for most youths—had especial poignance for Eugene because his parents, with their characteristic disregard for conventional family feeling, were not even in residence at their summer home that year. They had gone to Europe, and Eugene and his older brother, Jamie, spent the summer vacation on their own. The mature Eugene O'Neill, writing what was ostensibly a tender, sentimental comedy in *Ah, Wilderness!,* drew a certain bitter pleasure from contrasting his own boyhood summers in New London with the sort of summers spent by his contemporaries, whose parents devoted themselves uncomplicatedly to each other and to their children. The family he particularly admired and envied, and the one he had in mind when he created the Miller family for *Ah, Wilderness!* was that of his friend Arthur McGinley, the son of his father's old friend John McGinley. It was John who, in 1883, had urged James and Ella to buy a house in New London.

Like Nat Miller in the play, John McGinley was the editor (and part owner) of a newspaper; he had helped found the New London *Day* in the late 1800's. Also like Nat Miller, McGinley was the head of a large family. It was not only Eugene, but his father as well, who regarded the McGinleys' cheerful domesticity with a kind of awe. Once, when visiting the McGinleys and observing the easy, close-knit camaraderie that existed among the parents and their seven sons and daughters, James was moved to confess to his old friend, "I may have made some money and achieved some fame, but you're the man I envy."

Whenever James appeared in New London in his perennial vehicle, *The Count of Monte Cristo,* he reserved a box at the Lyceum Theatre for the entire McGinley clan. The children would show up scrubbed, shining, and eager. Arthur McGinley saw the play nine times as a result of this family ritual.

As was characteristic of him in most of his plays, Eugene O'Neill used many actual names of the people connected with the era and locale about which he was writing, or names approximating them. Arthur, Tom and "Wint" (a nickname for Winthrop) were given to characters in *Ah, Wilderness!,* and a boy named Lawrence is mentioned but does not appear. All four names belonged to the McGinley boys. John McGinley's wife, Evelyn Essex, became Essie, and the daughter, Mildred, took her name from a girl O'Neill had known and remembered in that era; her nickname, in the play and in life, was "Mid." O'Neill also threw in a policeman named Sullivan, who was actually Tim Sullivan, a well-known New London fixture. In the play Nat Miller's spinster sister, Lily, drew her name and much of her character from a spinster cousin of Ella O'Neill's named Lil Brennan. It was Lil who would protest to Ella and James that Eugene's reading should be censored, although in other matters she was inclined to take Eugene's part against his father. She recognized, for example, that James had made both Eugene and Jamie overdependent on him, and she felt that unless he changed his method it was unreasonable for him to expect them to display a mature sense of responsibility.

Richard Miller in *Ah, Wilderness!* reflected a number of Eugene's characteristics, but part of his personality was borrowed from a contemporary named Charles (Hutch) Collins. When *Ah, Wilderness!* was produced, Arthur McGinley wrote O'Neill to tell him that he recognized his own family in the play. O'Neill, feeling that he might have embarrassed his old friend, wrote back that none of the characters were taken from

life. "They are general types true for any large-small town," he added, "but the boy does spout the poetry I and Hutch Collins once used to. . . ." Hutch shared with Eugene (and Richard) a passion for the works of such then-scandalous writers as Wilde and Swinburne, and both boys could recite long passages from the Rubáiyát of Omar Khayyám (from which work the play's title derives; O'Neill substituted "Ah" for "Oh" because he thought the former conveyed the requisite sense of nostalgia). And, like one of the Miller boys, the two teen-age boys believed that Oscar Wilde had been imprisoned for the crime of bigamy.

It was Eugene who guided Hutch's early reading, but he did not have to guide his flair for dapper living. Hutch dressed like a dandy and wore white flannels and a hat with a London label that was both the envy and the butt of his friends, whose parents referred to him as "Jerry Collins's damn fool." One of Hutch's less elegant friends once nailed the hat to a wall as a joke. Both Eugene and Hutch were often seen emerging from the New London library with stacks of books under their arms, evoking the bewildered respect of their less intellectual friends. One such friend, on being questioned about Eugene by a younger boy, responded, definitively, "Look—Gene O'Neill, he reads *deep stuff!*"

But the seventeen-year-old Eugene, like Richard Miller, had his lighter, boyish side too, though in later years he was inclined to deny it. While he expressed his contempt for the stuffiness of New London, he did participate with boyish pleasure in the traditional Fourth of July celebrations, which he later described in *Ah, Wilderness!* The celebrations, with lots of fireworks, started at midnight on July 3 and lasted until midnight of the Fourth. But Eugene marked the holiday with his friends rather than with his family, recognizing that neither his mother nor his father was interested in or capable of the kind of cheerful family give-and-take that pervaded the McGinley—and the Miller—clans.

Eugene O'Neill was never to be far from the sea, and the sense of its presence pervaded many of his plays. Here, as a boy of ten, he sits on a rock by the shore at New London.

Eugene also took a boyish delight in listening to the popular nickelodeon tunes of the day, some of which turned up in *Ah, Wilderness!*—"Waiting at the Church," for instance, and "Bedelia." His nostalgia for the songs of the early 1900's lasted all his life; he could sing many of them from memory and sometimes did, in a dismaying croak.

O'Neill attributed his love of music, which included modern jazz and an indiscriminate smattering of the classics, to his mother's musicianship. She had studied piano for many years. But although he later acquired a sizable record collection and a fine phonograph, nothing could send him into quite the same transports as the tinny sound of a nickelodeon playing the tunes of the early 1900's.

In 1906 Eugene's ideas, like Richard Miller's, came almost exclusively from books. In that year, Eugene did a good part of his reading in the apartment-office of a dashing New Londoner named Joseph Ganey, who was ten years Eugene's senior and a contemporary of Jamie's. Ganey had been a butcher and a coal dealer before he decided to become a doctor. Shortly after settling

down to medical practice and acquiring the nickname "Doc," Ganey, much to Eugene's admiration, made an impetuous trip around the world, during which he collected a number of first editions to add to an already sizable library. Doc Ganey refused to allow Eugene to take any of the precious volumes home with him, but consented to let him read as much as he pleased in the apartment. Often Ganey would return home at three in the morning from a night on the town to find Eugene poring over Wilde, Schopenhauer, Zola, or De Maupassant. From early adolescence, Eugene had been devouring the books in his father's library; every summer he read through the complete works of Victor Hugo and Alexandre Dumas, in addition to Dickens and Kipling. He also read the Irish romantic Charles Lever and the volumes of Irish history with which James's library was studded, as well as the philosophy of Emerson and the poetry of Scott and Byron—he could recite "Childe Harold" interminably. It was not until he had exhausted the supply of recognized classics in his own home that he approached Doc Ganey's more so-

phisticated library.

But while Richard Miller is depicted in *Ah, Wilderness!* as shocking his family with lurid and antisocial quotations from disreputable European authors, he is shown to be basically innocent and pure in heart; his "depravity" is purely intellectual. Eugene, on the other hand, was inclined to practice what he preached, and although he was naïve, he was not innocent.

Doc Ganey's "Second Story Club," an informal, raffish, preponderantly Irish organization that would have stood Richard Miller's hair on end, was a milieu in which Eugene felt at home. The club, which met in Ganey's second-floor rooms on Main Street to talk, drink, and play cards, was composed of a kind of avant-garde of New London and was regarded with horror by the respectable citizens of the town. Art McGinley, who was tall and lanky and was called "a left-footed Irishman" by his friends because his family was Episcopalian, has said, in recalling Doc Ganey, "We ate his food, drank his liquor, wore out his carpets, read his books, and got free medical attention."

New London's harbor in Eugene's youth was still a port of call for sailing vessels as well as Sound steamers, but the yachts of the wealthy provided its chief traffic.

Unlike Richard Miller, who is shocked by his encounter with a prostitute in a shady hotel and resists her efforts to entice him to an upstairs room, Eugene was boastfully at home with the ladies of Bradley Street, a narrow avenue at the northern end of town that encompassed the flourishing red-light district of New London. Jamie had seen to his indoctrination, and the members of the Second Story Club saw to it that he continued his visits.

The brothels of Bradley Street, about a dozen in all, were housed in old, rickety, wooden structures which flanked the New London police station. This facilitated periodic police raids and generally made for the convenient working arrangement between the upholders of the law and the practitioners of vice that existed in many parts of the country. The girls would lean out of the windows and exchange small talk with the policemen while waiting for customers. When a house was raided and the prostitutes haled into court, the judge would ask, "Occupation?" and the customary answer would be, "Seamstress."

A description of the interior of a typ-ical Bradley Street brothel was given by O'Neill in *The Great God Brown* and was recognized with delight by some of his old companions in sin:

An automatic, nickel-in-the-slot player-piano is at center, rear [he wrote]. On its right is a dirty gilt second-hand sofa. At the left is a bald-spotted crimson plush chair. The backdrop for the rear wall is cheap wallpaper of a dull yellow-brown, resembling a blurred impression of a fallow field in early spring. There is a cheap alarm clock on top of the piano. . . .

"Here comes the kindergarten," the girls would call when Eugene and his young friends made their appearance. They usually arrived en masse, for reasons of economy: a round of beer was a flat one dollar, regardless of how many were in the group. At least two of the girls later gave up the profession to become respectable wives and mothers.

In distilling the character of Richard Miller, O'Neill also endowed him with an older and a younger brother (two others are mentioned, but do not appear as characters). Arthur Miller is two years older than Richard, a Yale undergraduate, and almost as innocent as Richard

himself. Eugene's brother was ten years older, an actor, a heavy drinker, a favorite on Bradley Street, and a man who knew all the Broadway gossip and could be amusingly informative about the least savory and most personal aspects of all the reigning soubrettes, a substantial number of whom had lost their heads over him.

Nat Miller, the father in the play, was also far from being a portrait of James O'Neill; Eugene, in his youthful resentment, compared his father very unfavorably with John McGinley, whom Miller more closely resembled. And yet, yielding to that inescapable bond of love beneath the resentment, the mature Eugene O'Neill endowed Nat Miller with two of James O'Neill's amusing and rather lovable traits. One was his conviction that "a certain peculiar oil" in bluefish had a poisonous effect on his digestion; it was a family joke that Ella served him bluefish under the guise of weakfish. (Ella herself was convinced that oysters were poisonous.) The other trait was his propensity to repeat stories of his boyhood and young manhood—illustrated in *Ah, Wilderness!* by what

29

was probably the only nontheatrical reminiscence in his repertoire: the story of how he had once rescued a friend from drowning.

But with that the resemblance between the warm, sentimental relationships of the Millers and the uneasy, confused relationships of the O'Neills ceased almost entirely. Mrs. Miller was nothing like Ella; she was more like Evelyn McGinley, who bore a physical resemblance to Queen Victoria and had all the maternal, bustling, good-natured officiousness that Eugene missed in his own mother.

And Eugene's youthful rebellion against the stuffiness of his surroundings was far more flagrant and sullen than Richard's. His own father's sense of paternal duty blew hot and cold by turns. During his adolescent summers in New London, Eugene was alternately berated for his lack of character and indulged with such expensive toys as a canoe and the rowboat in which he would float down the Thames at high noon, occasionally lying naked on the floorboards. There is nothing in Richard's character to suggest Eugene's profound love of the water and ships, nor does *Ah, Wilderness!* more than hint at the fact that the town in which it is set had a long maritime tradition. Eugene, however, was deeply conscious of this. He rarely missed watching the arrival or departure of the square-riggers that still, in the early 1900's, sailed with breathtaking beauty into New London harbor. He spent long hours talking to the ships' captains and crews, trying to recognize in them the romance he found in Jack London and Joseph Conrad.

Ella snobbishly disapproved of Eugene's acquaintances among the old salts who hung about the harbor, just as she deplored the fact that both Eugene and Jamie—and her husband, too, for that matter—seemed to prefer almost any environment to that of their home. She did not even derive much satisfaction from James's purchase of one of the first Packard automobiles in eastern Connecticut in a year when there were less than 80,000 motor cars in the entire country, for the kind of gay, duster-and-goggles outings indulged in by the Millers in *Ah, Wilderness!* was simply beyond the O'Neills. Ella was usually driven out in the car alone, and Eugene and Jamie, feeling very devilish, occasionally appropriated it for themselves. In recalling such times a year or so before he wrote *Ah, Wilderness!* O'Neill wrote a friend that he and Jamie "once got the car up to a mite over forty. A great day—from which the car never fully recovered!"

Although Eugene had a boat, the use of a car, and good clothes, he often had to borrow a nickel from one of his friends for trolley fare because his pocket money was so restricted; virtu-

Ella Quinlan O'Neill

ally his only source of income was what he earned from his father for trimming the hedge that surrounded the house— fifty cents for a good day's work. It was supposed to teach him the value of money. Yet in spite of restrictions, Eugene sometimes managed to pay his way into the Montauk Inn, the prototype for the tavern in *Ah, Wilderness!* and later for the off-stage inn in *A Moon for the Misbegotten.* The Montauk Inn, an inelegant establishment equipped with a nickelodeon and upstairs rooms, was located on the fringe of New London's most fashionable residential area. It was patronized by coachmen, farmers, and prostitutes like Belle in *Ah, Wilderness!,* who were partial to sloe gin. A pair of boxing gloves, said by the inn's proprietor to be those with which John L. Sullivan won his final bout with Jake Kilrain, hung behind the bar. (As it happened, Kilrain had finally been subdued by Sullivan in 1889 in a seventy-five round bare-knuckles bout.)

One of the inn's best customers was a pig farmer named John Dolan, who was a garbage collector on the side and who lived in an unbelievably ramshackle house on a disreputable piece of land that he rented from James O'Neill for thirty-five dollars a month. Besides pigs, Dolan also kept chickens, and these lived in his house with him, along with his two sons and two daughters. Tall, thick-set, and slightly round-shouldered, Dolan appeared abroad dressed in filthy overalls and a tattered brown hat. He could not write his name and he had a powerful fondness for the bottle; he also had a thick brogue, and a biting Irish wit that was the joy of his drinking companions. A thoroughly irreverent individualist, Dolan chose to be followed wherever he went by a huge Saint Bernard dog that adored him. Dolan, whom Jamie and Eugene observed with relish, became Phil Hogan in *A Moon for the Misbegotten.* Hogan's uproariously funny encounter with a young estate owner, whom O'Neill called T. Stedman Harder, was drawn from an account Eugene heard at first hand in the Montauk Inn.

Harder (who was modeled on Edward Stephen Harkness, the scion of an enormously wealthy family that summered in New London) complains to Hogan, in the play, that his pigs are infringing on the family ice pond, and Hogan gives him his comeuppance. (Ice from the pond was chopped in the winter and stored in an ice house to last through the warm weather; Harder did not care for the taste of pork in his drinking water, but Hogan accused him of knocking down his own fences in order to lure the pigs into the pond and give them pneumonia.) The same episode also occurs in *Long Day's Journey into Night,* but in that play it appears as exposition, with the names altered to Shaughnessy (for Dolan) and Harker (for Harkness). The ice pond in question actually belonged to Edward C. Hammond, whose summer estate adjoined Dolan's farm at the foot of a hill. But the Standard Oil background attributed to Harder-Harker in the plays belonged, rightfully, to the father of Edward Stephen Harkness, who helped John D. Rockefeller found the Standard Oil Company, against which Eugene, who fancied himself an anarchist, had a grudge. The Harkness summer estate, which in 1952 became a state park, was known as "Eolia"; it consisted of 235 acres running down to the Sound, a forty-two room mansion, formal gardens, and assorted barns, greenhouses, caretakers' cottages, and stables. It was run by twenty indoor servants, including three butlers, and an additional staff of forty groundkeepers, chauffeurs, dairymen, vegetable keepers, gardeners, and watchmen. The thought of grubby old Dolan standing up to and routing the inheritor of all this grandeur was enough to send the moody Eugene into gales of laughter that echoed in his mind for many years.

He was still thinking of Harkness and Dolan and the Montauk Inn when, in the early 1930's, he began writing a cycle of plays dealing with an American family over a period of more than a hundred years. In *A Touch of the Poet*, the only play of the cycle that he completed, O'Neill gave his rich Yankee villain still another variant of the name Harkness—calling him Harford, rather than Harder or Harker. O'Neill drew on his memory of Dolan, as well as of his own father, to create Cornelius Melody —a proud, ambitious, but defeated man, who drops his mask of pride to reveal himself as the son of a shebeen keeper. The incident in which one of Melody's Irish cronies kicks Harford's lawyer off his property is reminiscent of the scene in *A Moon for the Misbegotten* in which Phil Hogan expedites the departure of Harder from his farm. And Melody's tavern, though located near Boston in the year 1828, closely resembles in·atmosphere and clientele the Montauk Inn of New London in the early 1900's. Cornelius Melody's daughter, Sara, can be regarded in some respects as a refined version of Hogan's daughter, Josie, in *A Moon for the Misbegotten.*

By 1906 Eugene's predilection for types like Dolan and the prostitutes of Bradley Street, combined with his brother's reputation as a heavy drinker (even though Eugene had not yet started drinking heavily himself), made it difficult for him to have any communication with a girl like Muriel in *Ah, Wilderness!* The mothers of nice girls considered him anathema. One of the young daughters of a family with whom the O'Neills boarded from time to time when they had no cook has remembered being told by a friend, "The O'Neill boys are terrible. They're drunk and dissolute." She has recalled with amusement that any girl who valued her repu-

James O'Neill

tation made it a point of giving both Eugene and Jamie a wide berth.

Ella and James were understandably chagrined, yet James himself compounded the difficulty by warning parents to keep their daughters away from his sons; he thought it his moral duty to caution any of his friends who had impressionable daughters about his sons' profligate habits. Ella, on the other hand, professed to consider none of the New London girls good enough for her sons.

Ella kept mostly to her house, though she occasionally entertained and visited her nearby relatives, the Brennans and the Sheridans. When she was on morphine, she was not fit for social intercourse, and when she was between cures, she was too self-conscious and apprehensive to be sociable on a large scale. Her

relatives, unaware of what really ailed her, attributed her aloofness to snobbery. They also thought her vain, for she wore fifty-dollar French corsets and rarely went abroad without an expensive hat and a thick veil. The veil was attributed to her vanity of her smooth, white complexion, which she did not wish to be coarsened by sun or wind, but actually may have been used by her to hide the unnatural, morphine-induced brightness of her eyes.

Though considered snobbish by her own kin, Ella was in turn snubbed by the elite of New London, who were inclined to regard the O'Neills as something not far above riffraff. Their attitude had nothing to do with Ella's drug habit, which was a carefully kept secret; it was, rather, the unsavory combination of James's shanty Irish background, his career as a "road" actor, and his unpretentious mode of living that put off such leading New London families as the Chappells. Eugene resented the Chappells for snubbing his mother, although he was content to mention them only in passing instead of giving them the sneering, full-dress treatment he reserved for the Harknesses. In *Long Day's Journey into Night,* he calls the Chappells the Chatfields; and Mary Tyrone, who represents Ella O'Neill, refers to them, after they have driven past the Tyrone house and bowed formally to James Tyrone, as "big frogs in a small puddle." The reference has been cheerfully acknowledged by one of the younger members of the family, who has expressed regret at the narrow-mindedness of New London society in the early 1900's.

Mrs. E. Chappell Sheffield has recalled that her mother, returning in her victoria from a drive which took her past the O'Neill house, once remarked, "My, I certainly had a sweeping bow from James O'Neill." But, Mrs. Sheffield added, her mother would not have dreamed of calling on Ella—and Ella, restricted by protocol from calling first, had to swallow the affront.

"We considered the O'Neills shanty Irish," she observed ruefully, "and we associated the Irish, almost automati-

The O'Neills' New London home was a modest cottage on Pequot Avenue. James called it "Monte Cristo" cottage.

cally, with the servant class. As a matter of fact, I remember being very upset when I first started going to church—my father became a Catholic convert—and I recognized only servants in the church. 'Why do we go to the Irish Church?' I remember asking my mother, to her embarrassment. We were among the few Catholic families considered acceptable."

O'Neill, visiting Doc Ganey some years after he had achieved fame as a dramatist, told his old friend, "You know, I always wanted to make money. My motive was to be able, someday, to hire a tallyho and fill it full of painted whores, load each whore with a bushel of dimes, and let them throw the money to the rabble on a Saturday afternoon; we'd ride down State Street [New London's main thoroughfare] and toss money to people like the Chappells. Now that I've made as much as I need, I've lost interest." But the insult still rankled many years later; otherwise O'Neill would not have written so virulently of Cornelius Melody's hatred for the Yankees who snubbed him.

Eugene O'Neill spent little time in New London during the next six years. In the fall of 1906 he went to Princeton University, where he idled away most of his freshman year in what he later called "general hell-raising." Instead of return- *ing for his sophomore year, Eugene tried his hand at a routine clerical job in a New York City mail-order firm, then persuaded his father to give him a modest allowance to spend on a year of reading and acquiring "life-experience." Part of this life-experience resulted in his marriage to a nice New York girl, Kathleen Jenkins, who James, with no other justification than a natural suspicion of his son's stability, decided was a gold digger. Unaware that the girl was pregnant, James packed his son off to Honduras on a gold prospecting expedition. Eugene returned within a few months, without having acquired any gold, to find himself a father. But since James declined to be a grandfather, and since Eugene was wholly dependent on James financially, the marriage was soon terminated by divorce; and Eugene allowed himself to forget that he had a son or that he had ever had a wife.*

He was pressed, unwillingly, into a job as assistant manager with the touring production of The White Sister, *in which James was starred with the popular actress Viola Allen. But in the spring of 1910, Eugene left the company in Boston to sign, as an ordinary seaman, on a Norwegian bark bound for Buenos Aires. During the next two years he sailed aboard tramp ships and ocean liners, spent a period "on the beach" in Buenos Aires, and bummed around in* *waterfront saloons in Liverpool and New York. Out of these adventure-filled years —the most memorable in his life—came the material for his one-act sea plays, as well as for* Anna Christie, The Hairy Ape, *and* The Iceman Cometh. *Finally, after an attempt at suicide by drugs in a New York boardinghouse-saloon, O'Neill was reunited with his family in New London in 1912.*

The year 1912 was unquestionably the most significant of Eugene O'Neill's life, for it was then that he determined to become a dramatist. He made clear the significance of the date when he set the action of *Long Day's Journey into Night* in 1912 and underlined his dramatic intent by telescoping the events of several months into a single supercharged day. For some reason, however, he could not bring himself to reveal, either in the play or in any of the dozens of public statements he made about his beginnings as a dramatist, that the idea for his life's work was already formed in the summer of 1912. He always preferred to give the impression that the thought of writing plays did not enter his head until early the following year, when a breakdown in health forced him to take stock of his life. But a number of people who knew him well that summer have recalled that he was already making notes for plays, and several people have

Most of the mansions that Eugene envied were also located on Pequot Avenue. This was the home of Gordon Nonie.

remembered their shock and embarrassment at hearing Eugene say to his father, on more than one occasion, "Someday you'll be known as the father of Eugene O'Neill."

In August, 1912, when Eugene was nearly twenty-four, he became a reporter on the New London *Telegraph*. The newspaper, published daily except Sunday, had been founded in 1885 by Frederick B. Latimer, a man of liberal principles, integrity, and warmth, who as a friend of James O'Neill acceded to his request that Eugene be taken on.

The newspaper's staff consisted mainly of editors whose lively and divergent interests in foreign and political news gave the *Telegraph* a far more cosmopolitan flavor than its more reserved and circumscribed competitor, the New London *Day*. (The *Day* survives; the *Telegraph* is gone.) The *Telegraph* devoted considerable space to national news, particularly to news of New York City's underworld, and local coverage required only a small handful of reporters. The newspaper employed a red-faced printer's devil who spent most of his time in the Crocker House bar, when he was not fetching pitchers of ale for the reporters. There were no copy editors on the *Telegraph* and the reporters wrote their own headlines.

Reporters and editors worked in a musty little office and, like most newspapermen of the era, spent a good many of their working hours playing poker, gossiping, and making up for lost sleep. The reporter's desk was his card table, bar, and bed—and sometimes the place where he wrote a story. Such news as was covered ranged from fires and the fainting of fat women in the public square to the "classy scraps" that invariably took place among the celebrating sailors. "Brandishing a razor in one hand and a bedpan in the other, John Jones of no certain address ran amuck in the city hospital yesterday," was the lead of a typical story.

Staff members took their meals at a nearby all-night hash house which boasted a horseshoe bar flanked by mirrors. Jamie O'Neill often made this bar a port of call around three in the morning and could usually be counted on to give the reporters an impromptu performance highlighted by some graphic grimacing before the mirror.

Eugene found himself among friends at the *Telegraph*. He was particularly encouraged by Latimer, with whom he hit it off at once. "He's the first one who really thought I had something to say, and believed I could say it," Eugene once told the critic Barrett Clark. Clark, who was preparing a book about O'Neill in 1925, went to Latimer for confirmation: "As we used to talk together and argue our different philosophies," said Latimer (who had by that time sold out his interest in the *Telegraph*), "I thought he was the most stubborn and irreconcilable social rebel I had ever met. We appreciated each other's sympathies, but to each, in the moralities and religious thought and political notions, the other was 'all wet.'" (The year 1912 was a time of blossoming for the socialist idea: the illustrated socialist monthly *The Masses* was founded in New York; the millionaire Harry Payne Whitney bought the *Metropolitan Magazine* and installed the British Fabian socialist, H. J. Wigham, as its editor. Jack Reed was holding court for young radicals in Greenwich Village. It was a year when Eugene's political consciousness was at its most acute.)

Latimer considered Eugene the paper's cub reporter. He was impressed with Eugene's modesty, his courtesy, his wonderful eyes, and his literary style. "It was evidence at once that this was no ordinary boy," Latimer later recalled, "and I watched what he thought, wrote, and did with extreme interest. From flashes in the quality of the stuff he gave the paper, and the poems and play manuscripts he showed me, I was so struck that I told his father Eugene did not have merely talent, but a very high order of genius." Latimer found Eugene "emphatically different," and he admired his wit, his iconoclasm, and his

A mood of peace, not always to characterize their gatherings, exists in this 1900 photograph of the three men of the O'Neill family. James, right, sits on the porch with his sons: Eugene, left, then twelve years old, and Jamie, then twenty-two.

sympathy with the victims of man-made distress. He recognized Eugene's imagination and appreciated the vigor of his writing style, the heat of his spirit, and his scorn for commercial value or conventional fame. "If he could only be in one of two places in a town—the church or the jail—I know where I would find him!" Latimer summed up.

On the other hand, Eugene's city editor, Malcolm Mollan, was less inclined to be tolerant of his cub reporter's "genius." Mollan wore a silk hat and carried a cane. He cheerfully admitted that he was the sort of city editor who "faithfully lived up to the tradition that such a creature must cut the hearts of his subordinates to ribbons with malignant criticism." Recalling Eugene's five-month stint on the *Telegraph*, he wrote in the Philadelphia *Public Ledger:*

Time was when . . . I used to bawl out, "O'Neill!" and O'Neill would come to my desk and say, "Yes, sir."

"This is a lovely story about that Bradley street cutting! The smell of the rooms is made convincing; the amount of blood on the floor is precisely measured; you have drawn a nice picture of the squalor and stupidity and degradation of that household. But would you mind finding out the name of the gentleman who carved the lady and whether the dame is his wife or daughter or who? And phone the hospital for a hint as to whether she is dead or discharged or what? Then put the facts into a hundred and fifty words—and send this literary batik to the picture framer's!"

Mollan remembered Eugene's abashed, puzzled look as he carried away his story and "pulled his hair about his eyes while he tried to do a conventional, phlegmatic news item in newspaper style."

Mollan was aware that facts as such could not surprise Eugene and so did not interest him. "It was what they signified, what led to them and what they in turn led to, their proportionate values in the great canvas of life, that intrigued his rapt attention," wrote Mollan. "What difference did it make whether this particular brother of the ox, who had graven the proof of his upbringing on a woman's body, was called Stan Pujak or Jo Wojnik? What difference whether the knife found a vital or missed it by a hair? What O'Neill saw in the affair was just one more exhibit in the case of Humanity vs. the State of Things, another dab of evidence of the puzzling perversion of mankind, with its needless conflicts and distorted passions. He saw squalid bestiality usurping normal humanism in human beings. What he saw he wrote, that others might see. He had to."

Eugene realized that he was misplaced as a news gatherer. "I was a bum reporter," he told friends complacently in later years. Some of his fellow reporters on the paper would have agreed. At least one of them, in fact, later recorded his opinion that Eugene was "The World's Worst Reporter." Under that headline, nineteen years later, Robert A. Woodworth, then writing for the Providence, Rhode Island, *Journal*, recalled that Eugene would sit in a corner of the city room smoking and dreaming while other members of the small staff "ran their legs off."

"Hey, Mal, when is that guy going to get busy and do some work?" Woodworth would ask city editor Mollan in disgust. He has added that "as far as any of the crowd can remember, he never typed a thing in the late lamented *Morning Telegraph* office which savored of genius."

One of the stories Eugene covered, and for which he did manage to get the facts, concerned the arrival in New Lon-

The happy family of Ah Wilderness! *(above, with George M. Cohan as the father in the original production) was modeled not on the O'Neills but on their friends the McGinleys. But there was much of O'Neill in the seventeen-year-old Richard Miller.*

don on August 17, 1912, of Theodore Roosevelt. The story is a good example of his newspaper style:

Colonel Theodore Roosevelt, who is jocosely described by various pet names ranging from Bwana Tumbo to Chief Running Bull, passed through here on the eastbound limited at 3:38 yesterday afternoon and his presence in a Pullman car at the Union Station drew a crowd of 150 people. The colonel was distinctly visible from the platform and he bowed de-e-e-lightedly to the onlookers. He did not offer to come to the car vestibule at first.

Among the assembled throng was the rotund and genial Attorney Thomas F. Dorsey, who made the acquaintance of Colonel Roosevelt some years ago when his train passed through here. Teddy wasn't going to get away from New London without a handshake from somebody, not if Mr. Dorsey knew it. So the amicable disciple of Blackstone drew an engraved calling card from his pocket, carefully dusted it off and marched in with it to the hero of the jungle. The awestruck crowd without the portals watched the colonel accept the proffered pasteboard and give Mr. Dorsey the glad mitt.

But if Eugene did not exactly distinguish himself as a news-hound, he did earn a local reputation as a sardonic poet by his contributions to a column called "Laconics," which appeared on the editorial page of the *Telegraph* and consisted of contributions from various members of the staff. The column, which varied in form from day to day—sometimes it was a string of topical jokes, sometimes anecdotes, and sometimes caustic editorial comment—was usually written in a humorous vein. Eugene's contributions were invariably in the form of poetry. His untitled poem ("With apologies to J. W. Riley") which appeared not long after Roosevelt's visit, is typical:

Our Teddy opens wide his mouth,
N'runs around n'yells all day,
N'calls some people naughty names
N'says things that he shouldn't say,
N'when he's nothing else to do
He swell up like he'd like to bust,
N'pounds on something with his fist
N'tells us 'bout some wicked trust,
I always wondered why that was—
I guess it's cause
Taft never does. . . .

Eugene's hours on the *Telegraph* were from five in the afternoon to one in the morning, and he worked on Sundays to help get out Monday's paper. He would ride to work on a bicycle, presumably to save trolley fare, although cycling was a popular means of transportation even among businessmen at that time. One of his poems for "Laconics," after enumerating the pangs felt by Caesar, Joan of Arc, and Napoleon in their various hours of trial, ended:

I grant you their sorrows were great
and real
But comparison makes them light
With the gloom I feel as I ride my
wheel
To work on a Sunday night.

His salary was twelve dollars a week, and there was an unconfirmed rumor around the *Telegraph* office that it was paid by James.

Art McGinley, Eugene's closest friend in New London, was also a reporter on the *Telegraph*, despite his father's association with the *Day*. (McGinley, who was to remain a newspaperman, had worked first on the *Day* and later went on to the Hartford *Times*, where he became sports editor, a job he still holds today.) Eugene and McGinley would often go out drinking together on their days off, or after work.

"Gene and I wanted to drink America dry," McGinley has said, referring to

O'Neill dramatized the tragic decline of his brother Jamie (above, at eighteen) in A Moon for the Misbegotten. *Franchot Tone (right, center) played the role in the Broadway production of 1957.*

those days. In the bars of New London, particularly two called McGarry's and Neagle's, in which Eugene and McGinley spent a good part of their salaries, Eugene enjoyed holding forth on anarchism, Irish kings, and Irish independence. They did not lack female companionship, but the girls Eugene took out were usually of the sort classified by Arthur, in *Ah, Wilderness!*, as "fast Janes."

It had been three years since Eugene's last encounter with a respectable girl (now his ex-wife), and the consequences of that romance had not inspired him to try again. He avoided the nice girls of New London, which was not so difficult as it might have been, since the parents of most of them considered him pure poison and warned their daughters to avoid him. Notwithstanding his reputation, Eugene was just as attractive to nice girls as to the type he felt more comfortable with. His dark good looks, his shyness and apparent gentleness, his quality of seeming to suffer from some deep, unfathomable wound, were irresistible in themselves. These attractions, coupled with his sinister, if inexplicitly detailed, reputation and his status as a

divorced man with a child, made him an object of infinite glamour and desirability, except to the most timorous. And there were a number of distinctly untimorous maidens in New London. Luckily for most of them, Eugene held idealistic views about the girls he classified as "nice."

Toward the end of September, 1912, Eugene met the girl who, exactly twenty years later, was to serve as the model for Muriel McComber, the young heroine of *Ah, Wilderness!* Although Eugene himself was nearly twenty-four, and by this time quite a different sort from the Richard Miller of his play— and the girl was three years older than the fifteen-year-old Muriel—their romance had very much of the same breathless, innocent quality with which O'Neill tenderly imbued the relationship between Muriel and Richard. The clandestine meetings, the parental disapproval, the exchange of notes through an intermediary, the earnest plans for a distant marriage—all were nostalgically recalled elements in Eugene's courtship of the girl he fell in love with in the early fall of 1912.

Her name was Maibelle; she was tall and slender, with long, light brown hair, large blue eyes, a peaches-and-cream complexion, enchanting dimples, and a soft, appealing voice. In the opinion of Doc Ganey, a connoisseur, who has recalled observing Maibelle one day as she stooped to make a graceful adjustment to her garter, "She was beautiful." Maibelle's father, a captain and master diver who had salvaged many wrecks off the coast of Connecticut, later shifted to running a profitable general store in New London. (Muriel McComber's father, in *Ah, Wilderness!*, is the proprietor of a dry-goods store.) Maibelle's family, who lived a street away from the O'Neills, was eminently respectable and had been casually acquainted with the O'Neills for many years.

"I was terribly impressed with Eugene," Maibelle has recalled. "Aside from his being so handsome, he was vastly sophisticated—and, of course, I knew that he had been married and had a child. I also remember that he was always short of cash, and didn't dress especially smartly, but he was never sloppy."

It is easy to understand Eugene's

fascination for a sheltered young girl like Maibelle; the actress Lillian Gish, who became a friend of O'Neill's many years later, has remarked that *she* found it "terribly impressive" to learn of all the things he had done before he was twenty-four and "how fully he had lived at such an early age."

Although Maibelle was more than willing to be in Eugene's company, she quickly found that her family was far from happy about the relationship. Maibelle was hurt and bewildered by their attitude. She found Eugene gentle, well-mannered, and considerate. He was always sober when she saw him, and she could not understand why James O'Neill thought it necessary to warn her father to keep her away from Eugene. When she heard that James had told her father she was too good for Eugene, that he was a "no-good, drunken loafer," it simply drew her closer to him, for she was absolutely convinced that there was no truth in James's statements. Maibelle was an intelligent and sensitive girl, and she was also surprisingly free of small-town prejudices and self-confident enough to trust her own judgment. Even when James, trying to enlist the help of Maibelle's mother in breaking up the romance, told her that Eugene "fell for every pretty face he saw," Maibelle refused to believe any bad of Eugene.

Since any appearance in a public place was instantly reported as scandal and stirred up Maibelle's family anew, their dates consisted mostly of quiet walks on the outskirts of town. "Once we went together to the Lyceum Theatre to see *The Bohemian Girl*," Maibelle has recalled, "and my family was so incensed, we swore off public appearances." They had very few close friends in common who were willing to flout public opinion by entertaining them together, but Eugene's boss, Frederick Latimer, and his wife were among those willing to take the risk. The Latimers had them to dinner a number of times, and a friend who lived up the Thames, near Norwich, also risked censure by inviting them to his home once or twice.

Their relationship, as Maibelle has re-called it, was conducted largely on an intellectual plane, for Eugene could not help proselytizing and Maibelle was an avid pupil. He instructed her in what to read and presented to her, as his first gift, a copy of *Thus Spake Zarathustra*. Maibelle not only read and labored to understand the book, but tried to persuade all her friends to read and accept it. This was one of the things that early in her acquaintance with Eugene most shocked and upset her family.

Eugene continued to present her with books. He gave her volumes of Schopenhauer and Oscar Wilde, and she dutifully read through them and discussed them with him. The two wrote each other several letters a day, even though they were going to meet later on. Most of the notes, far from being love letters, dealt with the contents of the books Maibelle was currently reading under Eugene's supervision. In his notes, Eugene would ask her to pay special attention to one or another passage, or he would interpret some bit of philosophy he thought she might misunderstand.

All of the love poems that he wrote for "Laconics" were written with Maibelle in mind. "Only You," which appeared a few days after he met her, is typical:

We walk down the crowded city street
Thus, silently side by side
We loiter where mirth and misery meet
In an ever refluent tide.

You thrill with the joy of the passing throng
Or echo its weary sighs
You gaze at each face as it hurries along
—But I only see your eyes—

I only see your eyes, my love,
I only see your eyes
For happiness or misery
Are only real when seen by me
Reflected in your eyes. . . .

Eugene and Maibelle rarely quarreled and were nearly always happy and at peace together. Because he never showed Maibelle his brooding, somber side, or breathed a hint of the painful relation-ship with his parents and brother that he later portrayed in *Long Day's Journey into Night*, she was startled by the revelations of that play.

"I have no recollection of Gene being upset or disturbed about his family," Maibelle has said. "He never gave me the impression that he resented his father, and even took it calmly when James O'Neill warned my parents against him."

Somewhere toward the middle of October, 1912 (not August, as *Long Day's Journey into Night* indicates), Eugene developed a bad cold, which he attributed to having been caught in a downpour while riding his bicycle to work. Unable to shake it off, he gradually developed a dry cough, fever and chills and night sweats, and had to go to bed. Although he could not report for work, he continued to write poetry for the "Laconics" column. One of these contributions, "The Call," published in November, indicated the restlessness that his prolonged illness inspired:

I have eaten my share of "stock fish"
On a steel Norwegian bark;
With hands gripped hard to the royal yard
I have swung through the rain and the dark.
I have hauled upon the braces
And bawled the chanty song,
And the clutch of the wheel had a friendly feel,
And the Trade Wind's kiss was strong.

So it's back to the sea, my brothers,
Back again to the sea.
I'm keen to land on a foreign strand
Back again to the sea.

For a few weeks, there was no suspicion that Eugene had tuberculosis, and Ella made frequent references to Eugene's "bad cold," which would soon clear up. But here, all factual resemblances to *Long Day's Journey into Night* cease for the moment. Jamie was not even at home at the time—he had gone to a sanitarium to take one of his periodic Keeley cures—and James was in New York, except for weekends, mak-

ing the motion-picture version of *The Count of Monte Cristo* for Daniel Frohman, who, with Adolph Zukor, had begun operating the Famous Players Film Company. Eugene was treated by two doctors, both with excellent reputations, one of whom was the distinguished chief of staff of New London's Lawrence Memorial Hospital. By November 15, his condition had been diagnosed as pleurisy, and Eugene was devotedly being taken care of by a registered nurse he himself selected and who came to live in the house.

The nurse, whose name was Olive, has said, without rancor, "I think Gene must have been out of his mind when he wrote *Long Day's Journey into Night*."

Olive, who had patience, understanding, and a sense of humor, was about the same age as Eugene and had known him casually for many years. She was called on the case by Dr. Harold Heyer, who was assistant to New London's leading surgeon, Dr. Daniel Sullivan. Since both doctors were regarded highly, they bear no resemblance to the "quack," Dr. Hardy, whom the playwright described as having taken care of him. There *was* a New London doctor who was known as the town quack, and to whom O'Neill may have been referring

in *Long Day's Journey into Night;* he would visit his patients on a bicycle and his fee was twenty-five cents. Local wags referred to him as "Bicycle Joe." Stories of how he opened boils with a penknife and allowed children to die of ruptured appendix were legion in the town, and it is conceivable, though unlikely, that Ella went to him for morphine prescriptions.

Dr. Heyer ordered Eugene to bed when he developed fever and suggested that a nurse attend him. Eugene asked him to send for Olive, in preference to a stranger.

"At first Gene was very ill with what we thought was a bad cold," Olive has recalled. "He had a high fever and had to stay in bed and have cold bed baths to bring his temperature down. He was very shy and modest, and I had to put him at ease when I bathed him by repeating what I had often heard my nursing superintendent say to patients: 'I think no more of washing a back than of washing that door.' I stayed with him all the time except for the four hours I had off every day. He was very sick. He coughed a lot and developed fluid in his right lung. Dr. Heyer, who paid daily visits, called Dr. Sullivan to draw off the fluid with a hollow needle. He had to puncture the lung through the chest to

do this. It was terribly painful, but Gene was very brave; there was hardly a grunt from him."

Once the liquid had been drained, Eugene felt much better. His fever went down and he was allowed to get out of bed and sit in a chair facing the sun. But he had to rest a great deal, for he was subject to hemorrhages. Tuberculosis was still not mentioned as a possibility by Dr. Heyer or Dr. Sullivan.

Eugene occupied the front bedroom on the second floor, which overlooked the Sound. Olive had a room directly across the hall. "Gene had the best room in the house," she has recalled. "He wrote a lot in bed and read a great deal. He was working on plays; I remember his showing me snatches of dialogue and sketches of characters and notations about stage settings. There was a description he read me of a character called Chris. He told me that he had gone to sea partly because he had thought he might want to write some day, and it might be a way to get material. He kept his notes in one of those old-fashioned bureaus that had divided drawers. I thought he was a brilliant boy but a little warped."

Olive told Eugene that she felt a lot of his ideas for plays were "immoral."

"You are so naïve," replied Eugene.

". . . to face my dead at last and write this play—write it with deep pity and understanding and forgiveness for all the four haunted Tyrones." Thus wrote O'Neill in 1941 of himself and his family, whom he would call the Tyrones in Long Day's Journey into Night. *The play was given a brilliant production on Broadway in 1956, with Florence Eldridge and Fredric March playing O'Neill's parents, Bradford Dillman as Edmund (Eugene), and Jason Robards, Jr., as brother Jamie. The photograph on the opposite page shows the principals in that order, left to right. In 1946 O'Neill posed for this heretofore unpublished photograph by Erwin Blumenfeld, one of his last portraits and a memorable one.*

"If I didn't want to be polite, I'd say stupid." Having discovered Olive's weak spot, he pressed his advantage.

"Gene tried his best to shock me by telling me about his love affairs in New York and Buenos Aires and about the derelicts he had lived with on the waterfront," Olive has said. "He tried to make me feel uneasy, and now and then he succeeded. Later, other girls told me how he used to try to scandalize them."

Eugene at this period was intensely hostile toward his father. The complexity of his conflicting and constantly shifting emotions toward James defy rational interpretation.

"The Old Man and I got to be good friends and understood each other the winter before he died," Eugene wrote Art McGinley in 1932, just after he had drawn an idealized James in *Ah, Wilderness!* "But in the days [1912] you speak of, I was full of secret bitterness about him—not stopping to consider all he took from me and kept on smiling."

"Gene told me he resented his father," Olive has said. "He never said anything nice about him. He blamed him for the way he was dragged around as a child. But Mr. O'Neill seemed to be genuinely concerned about Gene. Of course, he was always a little theatrical. When he arrived home for the weekend, he would step out of his horse-drawn hack and come up the front steps with his arms flung wide, expecting Mrs. O'Neill to rush into them in greeting, which she did. Then he would go straight up to Gene's room."

"How are things going, son?" James would ask.

Eugene would mumble something and turn his back on James. He never invited him into the room. James would hesitate in the doorway, looking worried and uneasy. With his own robust constitution—he still liked to brag that he had never been sick a day in his life—he was always a little contemptuous of the physically weak or broken.

The tension between them was plain to see. One Sunday, Olive heard Eugene ask his mother, "Has the Irish peasant gone to Mass?"

Contrary to O'Neill's description of James Tyrone, who is pictured as being negligent about the formal observance of religion, James attended Mass every Sunday at Saint Joseph's Church. Ella's relatives, in fact, were constantly after James to bring Ella with him to church, but they had long since given up on Eugene.

But another aspect of James's character—the stinginess, on which his son harped in *Long Day's Journey into Night*—is more difficult to evaluate. It is clear that James did not try to cut corners on medical expenses for Eugene during the early stage of his illness, but whether or not he stinted on domestic help cannot be resolved. Ella's relatives have claimed that the O'Neills often brought well-trained servants with them to New London from New York, and it is reasonable to suppose that when no servants were in evidence their absence was due, not to James's tight-fistedness, but rather to Ella's inability to manage. As for James's concern with turning off lights in order to save on electricity— constantly reiterated in the play—this was a crotchet of a great many householders in the 1900's. In an era when a pound of ham cost seventeen cents and a pound of the best tub butter cost thirty-two cents, and when a family of four was used to dining very well at home for sixty dollars a month or less, the monthly charge of between seven and ten dollars for the newfangled commodity, electric light, seemed to be out of all proportion. There were few heads of families who did not feel, with James, that they were being duped into making the electric light company rich, and it was customary to burn only those lights which were essential to illuminate a small, specific area.

At this time James considered himself in a precarious financial condition. Actually he was worth somewhere between one hundred and two hundred thousand dollars in cash and real estate. But even though there were no taxes to speak of in those days, his expenses were heavy because of repeated outlays for Ella's medical care. His huge income from his great vehicle was at an end, for he knew he was too old ever to play Edmond Dantes again. In addition, he had just learned that because a competing company had come out with a three-reel *Monte Cristo* photoplay, his five-reel version could not be widely released; there just was no market for two *Monte Cristo* movies.

"I remember how bitterly disappointed Mr. O'Neill was," Olive recalled. (Although it was advertised as the first feature-length film ever produced in the United States and was shown in a few theaters that had not taken the competing movie, James O'Neill's *Monte Cristo* was soon withdrawn.)

It is true that James had accepted a role in a projected Broadway play, for which his salary was to be four hundred dollars a week, but he had no guarantee that it would be a success. He was convinced that his earning days were at an end, and since neither of his sons was able to support himself, he saw the poorhouse lurking in wait for him.

For Eugene, the crux of James's penury seemed to revolve—if the playwright's preoccupation with it in *Long Day's Journey into Night* may be used as a guide—on James's wish to send him to a state farm to be treated for tuberculosis. In the play, Edmund Tyrone becomes almost inarticulate with rage at the thought that his wealthy father is going to allow him to be a charity patient. In this one instance, paradoxically, Eugene chose to distort the truth in his father's favor. (Although the play indicates that James was shamed by his son into sending him to a heavily endowed semiprivate sanatorium, the fact is that James *did* send Eugene first to a state farm. As it turned out, Eugene was to spend only a short time there, and none

of his relatives or friends ever knew about it; he was transferred, after two days, to the Gaylord Farm Sanatorium, which resembled the description given in *Long Day's Journey into Night*.)

The doctors first suspected that Eugene had tuberculosis at the end of November. His condition became a little worse, and his doctors began making tests. Within a few days the fact that Eugene had tuberculosis was confirmed.

His case was not severe, the doctors said, but it was advisable for him to go to a sanatorium. He met Maibelle that evening and told her about it.

"It didn't occur to me to be frightened of contagion," Maibelle has said, "and I kept seeing him for a while, whenever he was well enough to get out of bed." Early in December, however, Maibelle left for a trip to Florida with her family.

Eugene grew depressed. Late in November he wrote a sad poem called "The Lay of the Singer's Fall," in which he described a gifted youth whose spirit was plagued by the devil of doubt: first his faith, then his heart, then his soul died.

"When Truth and Love and God are dead
It is time, full time, to die."

says the Singer in the last stanza.

On December 9, a Monday, Eugene's signature appeared for the last time in the *Telegraph*, at the end of a poem called "To Winter":

"Blow, blow, thou winter wind,"
Away from here,
And I shall greet thy passing breath
Without a tear.

I do not love thy snow and sleet
Or icy floes;
When I must jump or stamp to warm
My freezing toes.

For why should I be happy or
E'en be merry
In weather only fitted for
Cook or Perry [*sic*].

My eyes are red, my lips are blue
My ears frost bitt'n;
Thy numbing kiss doth e'en extend
Thro' my mitten.

I am cold, no matter how I warm
Or clothe me;
O Winter, greater bards have sung
I loathe thee!

On that same day, the *Telegraph* ran a story that began, "James O'Neill, the noted actor, will close his residence on Pequot Avenue today and will leave for New York, where he will begin rehearsing tomorrow for the wonderful scenic production, 'The Deliverer,' which will be played for the first time at the Century Theatre in about six weeks. . . ." (The title was subsequently changed to *Joseph and His Brethren*.) There was no mention of Eugene.

But on the afternoon of that same day, Ella went to stay with relatives in New London, and James, accompanied by Olive, took his son to the state farm where, he was more than half-convinced, he was leaving him to die.

After his transfer to the Gaylord Farm Sanatorium in Wallingford, Connecticut, O'Neill seriously began writing plays. He spent six months there before he was discharged as an arrested case, and, when he returned to New London, it was with his resolve truly fixed: he would become a dramatist. The romance with Maibelle ended soon after by mutual agreement. She had found a new love, and O'Neill was too preoccupied with his new career to cast more than a glance of nostalgic regret toward their brief idyll. But New London—the New London of Ah, Wilderness!, Long Day's Journey into Night, and A Moon for the Misbegotten— stayed in O'Neill's mind, always. It was there that he wrote his first important one-act play, Bound East for Cardiff, *there that he watched his father die six years later. It was to New London that his mother's body was brought for burial, and it was from New London that Jamie was carried away to a sanatorium to die of alcoholism. Though in later years O'Neill was often separated from New London by the width of a continent or an ocean, he returned there, always, in memory. It was the place where his dead were buried and where his youth, the only youth he had known, lived on.*

Timeless Teutons

An album by August Sander

PHARMACIST

TOWN OFFICIAL

APPRENTICE TEACHER

PIANIST

RESERVE OFFICER

PASTRY COOK

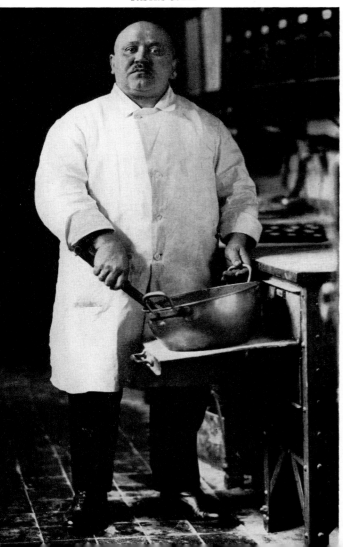

The German faces on these pages seem to tell of a time long past; yet neither the types they represent nor the individuals themselves are necessarily all extinct. The comfortable Rhenish family on page 41 looks like a period piece from the heyday of Kaiser William II; yet August Sander photographed it on a day near the old regime's end, and its posture may well have survived the fall. The fledgling teacher (lower far left, opposite) was recorded at the beginning of his career, at about the same time Hitler began his; and for all anyone knows, he may still be around somewhere in Germany, teaching yet another rising generation.

The maker of these pictures himself dates far back into the imperial era, yet he also survived several German upheavals thereafter. Reared in a Rhineland village to be a coal miner, young Sander resolved just before the century's turn to pursue his hobby of portrait photography and to try to make a living from it. In the old Germany's stratified, closed society, this made him an original; and he was to become even more original as a deadly commentator on that society, both in its flower and its subsequent decay.

To outward appearance Sander remained just another every-day photographer in the area around Cologne, busy posing burgh-ers, farmers, tradesmen in their Sunday best. Only once did he enjoy brief fame, when in 1929 he published a slender sheaf of what was to have been a much greater compilation of his local portrait prints under the title, *Portrait of Our Time*. But while critics applauded, the incoming Nazis soon after suppressed his work as "undesirable." It was not until thirty years later that the editor of the Swiss art magazine *Du*, haunted by the memory of that submerged sheaf, discovered that Sander was still alive, tracked down the octogenarian and his prints, and so launched a revival of his work.

The images on these pages make clear why the Nazis would have none of him. He peered all too sharply at the character of their country's life, with an unerring sense for the foibles and pre-tensions of class and caste. But what makes him more devastating is that he seemed to see with an innocent, simple eye leveled from within the heap. Here is no intellectual such as the George Grosz or Bertolt Brecht of the 1920's, deliberately out to satirize and maybe undermine the established order. Here, behind the camera, is the little man who was himself part of that order, and who is separated from it only by the click of his remorseless shutter.

That portly, elderly reserve officer at left above, stuffed in his aging regimentals for some memorial exercise between wars: how much his medals mean to him, while his seedy whiskers convey the irony of lost imperial glories. The glacial, overserious figure beside him could be the timeless archetype of German minor of-ficialdom. The musician below seems vaguely ill at ease despite his trappings of genteel *Kultur*—while on the other hand the gargantuan pastry cook stands rooted like some ancient tribal giant in the Teutonic landscape.

Overleaf, a between-wars legislator arises with celluloid collar and poised umbrella to defend the Weimar Republic against Hit-ler—maybe. A dispossessed grand duke dreams back to a hap-pier time, while four rather forlorn missionaries dream ahead to a better one. Oddities? Possibly. Yet in his shrewd search after the day's passing types, Sander looked far and fixed certain in-dividuals whose meaning, comic or tragic, or both, extends far beyond their own time.

LEGISLATOR

PASTOR'S WIFE

GRAND-DUCAL SERVANT

GRAND DUKE

EVANGELICAL CITY MISSIONARIES

The Imaginary Audience

Given the science of modern mass communication, we ought to know whether

anyone is there to get The Message from the Media. Yet often we do not:

the listeners have either disconnected their hearing-aids or stepped outside

No more elaborate equipment exists than that by which Americans communicate with themselves. Our access to information is easier, wider, and more frequent than that allowed to any other people, and we are ever eager to boast about it. We number the Mass Media among our most favorite institutions and, indeed, have granted them a power and penetration inconceivable to nations less in love with the sound of their own interior voices. Journalism has traditionally been called the "fourth estate," but it remained for twentieth-century America to clothe this aspiration in such substance that our politics can no more be imagined without our press than our commerce without our advertising.

For their annual diet of communication the American people pay some ten billion dollars. This is small enough in comparison with what they spend for food, housing, automobiles, or tobacco-and-alcohol, but large enough to rank among their major expenditures—about on a par, let us say, with health and medical care. This colossal bill goes to support some ten thousand newspapers, eight thousand magazines, eight hundred book publishers, four thousand radio stations, eight hundred television stations, and heaven knows how many miscellaneous public speakers, poets, skywriters, and other purveyors of the Word. Who listens?

In principle we ought to know the answer, since "communication" is now not only an imposing industry but an academic discipline, studied by scholars under grants from foundations and accepted in the universities, alongside "social relations," as part of the modern *trivium* and *quadrivium*. Serious examination of the Media has been going on intensively since World War II, and books on the subject—

By ERIC LARRABEE

with titles like *Mass Communication and Moral Responsibility*, or *Radio, Television, and Ultimate Truth*—have been pouring from the presses too rapidly for anyone but a professional to keep up with them. But, by a curious paradox, the Media and the scholarly students of them have each found their separate reasons for doing the same thing—for avoiding the question of whether the audience really exists.

The scholar is less interested in the audience than in the Media themselves. For one thing, he is mesmerized by their apparent size and power. For another, they seem to him to be in almost complete control of what the American public sees and hears, a matter on which the public itself seems to have little to say. This view is not only flattering to the Media but a potential source of still further income and reward; they can hardly be expected to deny possessing exactly the thing they are trying to merchandise. Both the commercial entrepreneur and the independent investigator have thus found an incentive to regard the audience as incomprehensible and inert, and they have reinforced the anxiety that lurks in every "communicator" as to whether he *has* an audience.

In everyone who faces the public there is something of Garry Moore, leaning toward the television camera with an arch "Hello, out there," as though to conquer his doubt. Each act of journalism is a stone dropped down a well in the hopes of hearing the splash, and what writer does not know the dead silence he must usually expect? A radio or TV appearance can echo into apparently total emptiness, and a magazine article that provokes a dozen comments—most of them irrelevant or ambiguous—is an exceptional success. On a larger scale, some of the most intensive efforts to convey a given idea to the American public have produced some of the most howling failures. Particularly in politics, it is notorious that the supposedly opinion-forming Media cannot put over a weak candidate or an unpopular issue.

Faith in the existence of the audience can reach its lowest ebb in the Mass Media themselves. Response is often in inverse relation to size: an article in a magazine which has a relatively small but contentious group of readers, accustomed to identifying themselves with what they read, may produce proportionately many more letters than in a publication whose readers run into the millions, but therefore think themselves individually insignificant. The more massive the medium is, moreover, the more private problems it has in visualizing its customers and the more reassurance it needs that the customers are there. No one can relate ten million people to anything he has personally experienced. When the audience gets that big, as in television, there is an increasing hunger for statistics about it, like the Nielsen and Trendex ratings, no matter how unconvincing they are.

Contrary to what you might expect, the large Media are thus more vulnerable than the small. They develop a kind of protoplasmic irritability to criticism. So much is at stake that they must watch the tiniest fluctuations in public taste with great care, and they will often make large decisions on the basis of what two or three "members of the public" say. In the early 1950's, when the shadow of the late Senator McCarthy still lay across the land, the entire television industry was terrorized by one single man, a grocery store owner from Syracuse, New York, named Laurence A. Johnson, who complained to the networks, agencies, and advertisers whenever a "controversial" performer appeared on

their programs. Johnson's extraordinary impact on the presumably all-powerful networks has been described in detail by John Cogley, in his *Report on Blacklisting* for the Fund for the Republic. Merely by being vocal and obstinate, to all intents Johnson became *the* public. "One complaint is enough, you know," as one producer said.

Those in authority well may realize, in the abstract, that they are equally responsible to the vast majority of their audience whom they never see or hear from, but the force of a face-to-face confrontation can drown out this awareness. I remember being surprised, on meeting the head of one network at lunch, to discover how concerned he was about the attitude of the people he met at dinner parties, who either disliked his programs, did not watch them, or both. Intellectually he knew that upper-class disdain for television was trivial and would pass, but the knowledge was not enough to protect him. The noise of his immediate audience was louder than that of his many million viewers.

Audiences are invisible until after the fact. The private persons who make them up have in common only the communication which they come together, for one instant, to receive. In other words, the American audience is imaginary to the extent that anyone who addresses it must imagine it into existence for himself. Neither the scholars nor the soap salesmen are likely to be of much help, for they acquire a vested interest in an audience only after it has been created.

The power of originality—in art, entertainment, or politics—is to assemble a new audience, by an act of the imagination, out of individuals who have hitherto not recognized themselves as related. Later will come the imitators to exploit the audience by sending similar sounding messages, until it becomes saturated with them and disintegrates. And later too will come the graduate-school specialists in "communications," with their butterfly nets and formaldehyde, to pluck the bright wings from the air and freeze and mount them, over the appropriate label.

A laboratory test of the Media's effectiveness was convincingly provided not long ago by the Texas oilman H. L. Hunt, who in 1951 established a tax-exempt, "educational" organization called Facts Forum to advance his ultraconservative views. According to the textbooks, one of the main obstacles to modern communication is its expense, but in Hunt's case this was no problem. His personal fortune was estimated at two billion dollars and his income at a million a week, in addition to which his contributions to Facts Forum were treated as tax-deductible, and he was able to get three million dollars' worth of radio and TV time for free on the grounds that his five nationwide programs were "news discussion." Facts Forum sent out sample "polls" to newspapers, published a monthly magazine, and sponsored neighborhood forums throughout the nation. But all to no avail. After five years of it, Hunt came to the conclusion that he was having no appreciable effect on public opinion, and he decided to drop the whole thing. As one of his associates put it, he "just got tired of useless and lost causes."

Hunt's rejection by his hoped-for audience can be explained by ineptitude and by the current of his times, which happened to be running against him, but it is less easy to explain in the light of academic theory. Theoretically, Hunt enjoyed the same advantages which make it possible for the masters of the Media (as described in the books) to exercise their sometimes benign, sometimes malevolent, sway. According to theory, communication is a linear, one-way process: "*Who* says *what* through what *channel* to *whom* with what *effect*"—to paraphrase Harold Lasswell, a pioneer investigator of these mysteries. The theory has little room in it for questions about what the audience will accept, or how one discovers this, or how the Media take account of it.

On this score, the egghead and his most extreme opposite in the marts of trade have an unwonted community of interest. Academic intellectuals are fascinated by the Mass Media in much the same way that they are fascinated by other manifestations of popular culture. The Media give them the impression of pursuing an activity somehow related to education, yet at what looks to them like a much lower level of quality and a much higher level of quantity—and making money at it, which is very annoying to underpaid professors. They find it difficult not to believe that some secret is being withheld from them, some magic formula for sugar-coating the bitter pill of knowledge which would enable *them* to reach an audience of millions. And who stands in their way but the illiterate gatekeepers, all the editors and publishers and network executives who so obviously—to an outsider's eye —determine what the public gets?

Thus the intellectual is predisposed to believe about the Mass Media the one thing their most venal custodians would like to have believed—namely, that the public can be manipulated. Advertising and public relations have nurtured an extensive doctrine which presumes the existence, or asserts it, of a technique by which an audience can be caused to do and think certain things it might not otherwise have done or thought; and one need hardly remark that belief in the efficacy of this technique is one of the products its practitioners are engaged in selling. But what is most distressing is the matching of this commercial claptrap to the prejudices of Academia, so that these two supposedly antipathetic groups—far from serving to correct one another—fall into happy accord over a set of thoroughly dubious propositions.

What they agree on is a model of communication in which information moves from a sender, through the Media (hence their name), to a receiver. This is a simple and convincing image, deriving much of its plausibility from gadgets like radio and the telephone, still to most of us the prime symbols of "communication." In fact it is not surprising that Communications Theory, so-called, as a "hard" science, took its start from the mathematical formulas which Norbert Wiener and Claude Shannon applied to problems of electronics in

1948. Subsequently these formulas became an academic fad, and the Theory was employed in numerous areas where it produced less fruitful results, but the minds of many specialists in "communication" still bear its mark. It leads them to the assumption, so fundamental as to pass almost unnoticed, that in the normal communications process the energy, initiative, and control lie on the side of the sender.

This has been called the Hypodermic Theory of Communication, and it has been the cause of much mischief. Some of the responsibility goes back to Norbert Wiener himself, who wrote about Mass Media in his *Cybernetics* only to deplore their lack of "feedback," or audience response; and at conferences on "communication" one is still likely to encounter the same notion of an apathetic and inarticulate public, which takes what it gets and has to like it. Unfortunately there is no quick and easy way of conveying to people who have no experience of it what the mass communication process is like, and how sharply it differs from this picture. Far from caring so little what the audience thinks, the mass "communicator" thinks about very little else. The size of his audience determines his income; its variations in behavior determine the limits of what he can and cannot attempt; the gift of its attention is his dearest prize; and the faintest sign of its boredom—just the touch of a yawn—is his worst nightmare.

You would never know this, however, to read the textbooks on Mass Communication. With an admirable skepticism, their authors have been hard at work tearing down the "democratic" pretenses which the Media like to hide behind. "We only give the public what it wants" is, of course, the age-old excuse for shoddiness and vulgarity of all kinds, and there is no trick in showing it up for the hypocrisy it so often is. But this entrancing side show has diverted attention away from the main event: it focuses concern on the overt intentions of the Media and their apparent content, and away from the question of which messages get through to the audience, and which do not, and why. If you assume the Hypodermic Theory to be true, then managerial control of the Media is bound to seem dangerously concentrated—as it did in 1947 to the Commission on the Freedom of the Press, under the chairmanship of Robert M. Hutchins, which was deeply disturbed at the decline in the number of newspapers and the increase of cities whose papers had no competition. This tells us little enough about the difference between good newspapers and bad, but about the way "news" is selected by the Media, it tells us virtually nothing at all.

Obviously the owner of a Mass Medium—or whatever the singular of that deplorable word is—can exert a certain leverage on his employees, but in practice this plays an insignificant part compared to the latter's considered judgment as to what the public will or will not like. That is the day-to-day job, the profession (or so they fancy it) of journalists, commentators, program directors, and all the rest of them; and to say that there is no "feedback" is to say that such people are either incompetent or ineffectual. They may be clumsy, venal, or sunk in vice, but in their way they must daily do as the artist must do, and make choices between different words, sounds, and pictures on the basis of what they think these will convey to somebody, however remote. Great poets need great audiences, as Whitman said, and even the most benighted "communicator" must also find his proper audience—if necessary, one as yet unborn—or court the dangers of sterility and antic posturing.

In 1948, the year after the Commission on the Freedom of the Press published its report, we were treated to a spectacular demonstration of how irrelevant its worries over concentration were. On November 2 there was a national election, the results of which had been confidently announced in advance by all of our freest and most original spirits. Walter Lippmann: "the Democrats cannot be serious about winning this election." Max Lerner: "if Truman is nominated, it will be as a gesture of party abdication and despair." Joseph and Stewart Alsop: "the problem is simply, who is to be boss, Dewey or the Congress?" Elmer Davis: "the Stop Truman movement has been successful. They can't stop him in July but they have made it certain that Dewey will stop him in November." *New York Post:* "Governor Dewey: When you become President . . . we will help you in every way to be a great progressive leader. . . ."

No degree of independence protected the commentators from being misinformed about the public. Nothing in the vast preponderance of pro-Dewey newspapers (almost 80 per cent of national circulation) enabled their owners to affect the outcome. President Truman and his audience (all 24,105,812 of them) turned out to have been in the most intimate communication by means which not only evaded nominal control but escaped the attention of the most observant professionals. The Great Information Machine had neither been listening to anybody nor talking to anybody. It had been talking to itself.

What had happened, and can happen again, was that assumptions about the audience had become self-confirming. People do not always tell you what they are listening to, or why. A writer may attract an audience by a particular tone of voice, and go on using it, though in fact his readers have long since ceased to care and stick with him despite, rather than because of, his style. Virtually every device for appealing to an audience is a literary convention, just as arbitrary as the detective story or *terza rima*, and observed only because both writers and readers find it useful. Joseph Alsop is among the best of our journalists, but his Cassandra-like prophecies are surely discounted by many of his readers.

Audiences get used to going along for the ride. Everyone can supply his own examples of a message received from the Media by "overhearing" it, on the assumption that it was meant for someone else. Most of us progressively acquire a sort of automatic gearshift, which allows us to lift material out of an information-channel without identifying ourselves with the people for whom it was intended. Similarly, anyone who insists on receiving all the messages that come his way, including the advertisements, is in our time likely to appear somewhat eccentric. I do not bear any resemblance, so far as I know, to the readers at whom *Vogue* magazine is directed, but I am unable to resist reading it, if only for the illusory sense that such a world of fuss and fantasy might exist.

Similar miscues and short circuits are a common feature of the communications trade. Messages have a dynamic of their own; some are inherently more potent than others and may even threaten—like the full-color nudes in magazines supposedly intended for camera fans—to take over the Medium that sends them. Once a Medium gets a name for reaching a certain audience, it tends to overaccumulate messages addressed to that audience. The Sunday *New York Times,* for example, has the reputation of being read by the out-of-town "buyers" in the wholesale garment industry, with the

result that its Sunday magazine gives the impression of being directed largely at consumers of women's underwear. Furthermore, a message can be sent through a Mass Medium to a very small group. The daily *Times* often prints large ads, paid for by ad agencies or the Media themselves, containing nothing but information about their success in selling ads and obviously intended for only a few dozen other people in the ad business. The same information could have been sent as easily—and a good deal less expensively—in a letter, but putting it in *The New York Times,* where a much greater audience can see and ignore it, is nonetheless the best way of getting it read.

Journalism as a whole—using the word to include radio and TV as well as newspapers and magazines—has developed an extensive armory of such arbitrary conventions for dealing with its audience. Most of them are based on the understanding that the American public demands the "news," and several of the most whimsical and inflexible deal with what is "news" and what is not. "News" is the rock-bottom raw material on which all other journalism rests; "interpretation" is possible only after the news has called it forth. Yet the typical news story is framed for a reader with the most odd and imbalanced needs. He seems to want certain facts over and over again, but he cannot bear having them put in context. "His intelligence is such," Douglass Cater writes, "that he must have it explained day after day who is Secretary of State, but, paradoxically, can be trusted to have highly complex issues described for him in a few terse phrases."

There would be nothing reprehensible about these formulas if they did not accumulate such power to distort and obscure the events they purport to describe. Mr. Cater, a Washington correspondent who has since become the first Professor of Journalism at Princeton, gives several horrendous examples in his recent book, *The Fourth Branch of Government,* of how reporters intervene in the creation of news and then, having done so, try to conceal that fact. Among them is a pair of headlines which appeared in *The New York Times,* three days apart, in the spring of 1955 during one of the Quemoy-Matsu crises. The first read: U. S. EXPECTS CHINESE REDS TO ATTACK ISLES IN APRIL; WEIGHS ALL OUT DEFENSE; the second: EISENHOWER SEES NO WAR NOW OVER CHINESE ISLES. Of the two stories underneath, neither contained a single indication as to who was the source of these awesome, and apparently authoritative, statements.

As it happened, the first had been set off at a background dinner held for a picked group of reporters by the then Chief of Naval Operations, Robert B. Carney, who was well known for his belief that war in Asia was imminent. Ten months earlier, at the time of Dienbienphu, he had, in fact, made a speech comparing the situation to Munich. No one could be expected to make sense of the *Times* headline without knowing this, or knowing that other members of the Joint Chiefs disagreed with Admiral Carney. But convention decreed that the reader should get the news, as we say, "straight." The source of the second headline had less obscure motives. He was, so Mr. Cater writes, "none other than the White House press secretary, James Hagerty, who attended a hastily called second background conference in order to repudiate the stories arising out of the first."

Mr. James B. Reston, chief of the *Times* Washington bureau, is the inventor of an engaging imaginary gadget called Uniquack, which reduces to simple English and its inner meaning such public documents as a letter from Eisenhower to Khrushchev. Mr. Reston has had much good sport with Uniquack, but one wonders how much of the *Times* front page could stand to be similarly processed. How many stories beginning, "Administration sources yesterday revealed . . ." should actually have read, "Last night me and the boys had dinner at the Metropolitan Club with Undersecretary Snodgrass, and he showed us a lot of memos we had no business seeing"? Lately the *Times* has been especially prone to personify something called the White House. "WHITE HOUSE DENIES . . ." says the front page on the day I happen to be writing this. Now either that is Jim Hagerty or it isn't, and Mr. Reston ought to be able to decide before he has still further fun at the expense of the President.

There is a Heisenberg Uncertainty Principle which operates in journalism just as regularly as in nuclear physics: the reporter himself has an impact, merely by his presence, on the fact he reports. The subtle artistic effects of "objective" journalism require a continual denial of this, but every now and then—as in the Khrushchev cross-country visit to this country—the illusion breaks down, with hilarious results. On Mr. Khrushchev's trip, in fact, the reporting *became* the event. The machinery had grown so cumbersome that it overwhelmed anything it came in contact with. Coon Rapids, Iowa, which normally telegraphs the rest of the world a hundred words a day, had to be equipped with twenty-four high-speed channels to handle an expected hundred thousand words an hour when the official party, which included 260 American newspapermen, arrived. The most newsworthy "news" event then took place when the latter arrived en masse in a barnyard and had certain barnyard materials thrown at them by their discommoded host, a man who thereby earned himself much public sympathy.

The danger is that the "news" (as Reuel Denney has suggested) may become a fantasy literature masquerading behind the techniques of documentary realism. We are used to consuming it in enormous quantities and letting it become, whether we want it to or not, at least the background noise to our sense of what is happening in the world. It has often been said that waves of crime and juvenile delinquency are the invention of newspapers, but this is equally plausible of the great international crises. Our journalism has difficulty in disconnecting itself from the momentum it lends to abstractions. The reporter must protect his sources since he will need them next week, but in the same sense he must protect the "news" itself, for he is committed to the proposition that something important has happened often enough to keep him employed. One cannot imagine Mr. Reston taking his space in the Sunday *Times* to say: "This week nothing of the slightest significance occurred," though obviously he often feels that way. Just as the hunger for active verbs —"U. S. SPURNS . . ." and so on—tempts the reporter to attribute dynamism and personality where none belongs, so the whole grand construction of communication feeds on crisis, and crisis piled on crisis, until it is a wonder anyone pays it any mind at all.

Communication is not a tube to pump information through. It is a net of connections as dense and delicate as the human nervous system; and, like the nerves, it can convey many impulses, many of them contradictory, in many directions at once. The audience comes to the Media for as many different reasons as it has members—to be diverted, to be reassured one is sane, to gossip, to be ennobled, to pass the time—and none is to be disparaged. The model of communication now so widely used makes not enough allowance for this complexity in the audience, for the subtlety and justice of its responses, even when it is bored or sleeping.

Communication serves society in much the same way that the nervous system serves the single animal. Its purposes are, as the specialist would say, "homeostatic"—they act, like the delicate fibers which preserve body temperature and chemical balance, to make certain we do not swing too far one way without being drawn in another. No specific organ of communication can be considered in isolation, apart from the role it fills and the demands the body politic may call upon it to meet. We do not always know what these are; we do not always know what is success or failure, or whether our own puerile messages—which we flatter ourselves the world cannot get along without—really deserve to be heard. Access to the system is anyone's privilege, but the fate of the message rests with the ever-changing audience.

When too much about him is taken for granted, the hypothetical reader or listener becomes a tyrant. Especially if he is assumed to be an idiot, he serves as an excuse for everything unadventurous and routine. "It is the conceptualized picture of the reader that governs our present-day journalism like some unseen autocrat," as Mary McCarthy has written. "He plays the same role the child plays in the American home and school, the role of an inferior being who must nevertheless be propitiated." The fault is not in monopoly, or the opacity of editors and network executives, but in a public dialogue that has become frozen and *pro forma,* yet is carried on by all parties, each on the assumption that the others demand it. What the audience does, under the circumstances, is what you might expect: it shows all of the outward signs of listening but has disconnected its hearing-aid; it has wrapped itself up inside a polite, attentive smile and vanished.

In the act of communication the audience is always imaginary, and should be. It is when we try to organize and dissect it, or rely on it, that the words dry up and the people in the back row start to fidget. If the public dialogue declines, as it is periodically bound to do, then it is not going to be revived by exhortation or by audience surveys that tell everything about the public except its as-yet-unsatisfied wants. The problems are aesthetic problems, and the answers will be aesthetic, too. The devices that bring new audiences into being are those, not of manipulation and analysis, but of art—of inventiveness and sensibility—and only by artists will they be responsibly employed.

This article, the third in a series by Mr. Larrabee, was preceded by his "The Wreck of the Status System" (November, 1959) and "The Cultural Class War" (January, 1960).

By JOHN CANADAY

From Salon to Cellar—and Back?

Few styles have fallen so far into disrepute as the once-prized academic art of the nineteenth century. Bad as most of it was, there are grounds for recalling some of it from exile

For the nineteenth-century public, a picture was art as long as it bore the solemn stamp of Salon approval. Jean Léon Gérôme's wonderfully pretentious version of the classic myth, Pygmalion and Galatea *(opposite), an academic exercise spiced with bourgeois eroticism, remained a collector's item even for art lovers with access to Daumier's murderous burlesque of the same subject (above).*

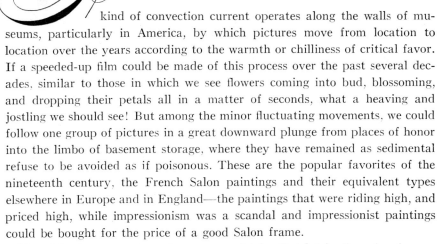

A kind of convection current operates along the walls of museums, particularly in America, by which pictures move from location to location over the years according to the warmth or chilliness of critical favor. If a speeded-up film could be made of this process over the past several decades. similar to those in which we see flowers coming into bud, blossoming, and dropping their petals all in a matter of seconds, what a heaving and jostling we should see! But among the minor fluctuating movements. we could follow one group of pictures in a great downward plunge from places of honor into the limbo of basement storage, where they have remained as sedimental refuse to be avoided as if poisonous. These are the popular favorites of the nineteenth century, the French Salon paintings and their equivalent types elsewhere in Europe and in England—the paintings that were riding high, and priced high, while impressionism was a scandal and impressionist paintings could be bought for the price of a good Salon frame.

No tables have ever turned more completely. But lately there has been a stirring within the depths. a quiet and half-surreptitious upward seepage of Salon painting from basement into backstair halls, into odds and ends of spaces not much visited. and occasionally even into the exhibition galleries proper. It is increasingly possible to see not only Cézanne, whom everybody knows, but also his contemporary Gérôme, whom everybody has forgotten although he was so well thought of during his lifetime that his objections to impressionism (he called it "filth" which only a "great moral slackening" could make acceptable) helped keep some extremely good pictures, including Cézanne's, out of the Louvre. It is possible also to see Renoir, whom everybody loves, on one wall and Bouguereau. whom everybody used to love, on another nearby. It is not yet safe to suggest that Renoir at his worst and Bouguereau at his best may have something in common, but in all probability

someone is going to open that sluice gate before long.

At present the safe attitude toward Salon painting is one of amused condescension. Even this is a step upward for the outcasts: horror and revulsion were obligatory only a few years ago. In the story of modern—that is, latter nineteenth- and early twentieth-century—art, the Salon painters have been presented as the Bad Guys and the impressionists, whom indeed they persecuted, as the Good Guys. But the defeat of the villains has been complete enough to satisfy even their bitterest enemies. Just why the undeniable faults and the possible virtues of Salon painting have been so jug-gled about takes a little explaining.

The Salon originated as an official exhibition in which ac-credited painters could present their work, summarize their theories, and introduce their protégés, usually by means of large demonstration pictures. The importance of the Salon in France, a country where art has always been part of the fabric of national life and where, until recently, the exhibi-tion of a picture could affect the prestige of the government, is hard to understand in a country where the most nearly comparable institution is the Automobile Show, and where the commercial dealer has taken over the function of middle-man between artist and public. The Salon still exists, in an abject and pointless way, but effectively it died of giantism in the nineteenth century.

Around a quarter of a million paintings must have been given official exhibition in France between 1800 and 1900, and as many more presented for exhibition but rejected by the juries. Most of them were, of necessity, bad or at best inconsequential, since there simply are not enough good painters working at any time to produce that many good pictures anywhere, not even in France. Ready to drop of its own weight, the Salon was given the *coup de grâce* by its own abuses. It became not only the annual testing ground for new talent and the prancing ground for established tal-ent, but also the torture chamber for any exceptional picture that happened to get in for one reason or another, as Manet's *Olympia* did in 1865.

The Salon juries were dominated by the pedants of the French Academy, an institution whose history in the nine-teenth century is appalling, whose practices were loathed by every artist and intellectual of much perception, and whose chairs continued to be coveted beyond all other honors never-theless. As one of the five branches of the Institute of France, the Academy of Fine Arts was nominally dedicated to the recognition of French genius and the fostering of the high-est achievements in art. In practice the Academy became a closed circle of conventional talents, of men skilled equally in the manipulation of trite formulas for painting and the manipulation of advantageous personal contacts. The situa-tion was deplorable, but it was also inevitable. Mediocrity rather than villainy accounted for the academic persecution

of painters who are now recognized as the great ones of the century; the academicians sincerely believed that they were defending the purity and sanity of art against the assaults of boors and madmen.

Genius being, by definition, original, its manifestations could hardly be perceived by a group of men in positions of entrenched privilege whose election to the Academy was part of the assumption that the formulas for great art had been crystallized once and for all. Delacroix, who was finally elected to the Academy when he was old, sick, and tired, and who continued to be snubbed by its officials even after

election, once said that an academician taught beauty as one teaches arithmetic. The Salons were made up of thousands of these exercises in addition and subtraction, hung frame to frame from floor to ceiling in vast halls through which the public thronged to admire or to deride, taking their cue from the critics—and to buy.

Painting became merchandise and the Salon became a gigantic salesroom. A painter who couldn't manage to get into it had little chance of selling his pictures for a decent price, or of placing them with a dealer, or even of getting them into another spot where many people were likely to see them.

55

urne-Jones's girls descending The Golden Stairs *were high fashion in 1880, but in 1912 Marcel Duchamp's multiple-exposure* Nude Descending a Staircase *changed all that.*

The Salon took on the nature of a life-and-death arena for the painter because he had become dependent upon a new kind of buyer. Before the nineteenth century the artist worked for small and cultivated groups of patrons, but this class had its head chopped off in the French Revolution. As the century coalesced into the great age of the common man, the painter had to find his living in the open market by appealing to an aesthetically ignorant public on other than aesthetic grounds. An ecstatic love affair developed between the affluent purchaser with mediocre taste and the skilled painter of mediocre conceptions. And the Salon was their trysting place.

Two considerations above all others attracted buyers. The first was slick technique, which made of the painter a kind of stunt man; the technical level of Salon painting was very high. The second was anecdotal interest. A painting had first of all to be an illustration, and a painter could base a long and successful career on a single anecdotal gimmick. The painter Vibert, for instance, who was a superb technician, devoted his talent to anecdote after anecdote after anecdote showing Roman cardinals as lovable old codgers in humorously undignified situations, or depicting young priests being naïvely taken aback by the worldly pranks of their parishioners (see his *The Startled Confessor,* on page 65). More "serious" painters inflated their anecdotes with sentimental moralizing and intellectual pretension. The typical Salon painting flattered the prospective purchaser by assuring him that his favorable response was the result of his moral probity, his intellectual acumen, and his cultural elevation.

Pictures like Gérôme's *Pygmalion and Galatea* (illustrated

on page 52) filled the bill on every score. The anecdote was ready-made, since the Pygmalion story has always been a good one. And as presented with all its pre-Shavian classical trappings, it also flattered the observer by assuming his familiarity with classical legend. This was culture. The fair lady, being naked for legitimate reasons, could be legitimately ogled. This was a pleasure. And Gérôme's impeccable technique was turned to a ravishing novelty effect: the statue-woman grades from luscious pink, where she has come to life (and has already started to work) down to pure white, where she is still marble. This was where the art came in, and what more could you ask? Daumier's hilarious burlesque of the subject (shown on page 53) suggests a disconcerting answer —yet a public with access to this cartoon continued to take Gérôme seriously.

Armies of nudes swarmed across the Salon walls, pretty girls without a stitch on but elaborately disguised by titles. A bourgeois society obsessed with the surface observance of a moral code unsympathetic to the display of the body found the most delicious release in artistic subterfuge. The Emperor Napoleon III himself bought Cabanel's provocative *Birth of Venus* out of the Salon of 1863, yet in 1865 Manet's *Olympia* was a scandal for its "indecency." Cabanel's Folies-Bergère beauty suggests one thing and one thing alone: even the official critics found her daringly "wanton." But since she was a Venus conventionally and very skillfully painted by a ranking academician, everything was all right. The culture more than made up for the wantonness, and the lines of the picture were found to be "of great purity," which helped. But Manet's masterpiece was compared to "high" game and the people who gathered around it, to morbid curiosity seekers in a morgue. This latter comparison was not far from wrong, since they had come to see a "dirty" picture, the critics having given this label to *Olympia* because the model was boldly and objectively painted as a Parisian courtesan, unabashed. Honesty was always a dangerous policy in the Salon.

The nude had been a standard test piece for centuries, but since art for art's sake did not interest the Salon public, and since the nude for the sake of the nude was morally suspect, the Salon painters invented a hundred ways to involve nudes or seminudes in acceptable anecdotal situations. Psychiatrists should have no trouble explaining why these females got into so many painted difficulties. They were always being sold into slavery while prospective buyers subjected them to such indignities as examining their teeth. They were often put to the torture—lashed to stakes and the like—and they languished in prisons on heaps of straw while coarse guards stood by indifferently. They couldn't so much as disrobe for a quick dip in a woodland pool without being taken by surprise. Naturally, they resented all this, and their expressions of outraged modesty allowed the observers in the Salon to combine perfectly normal sympathy for the poor things with equally normal but less open response to their charms. Every figure in history who could conceivably be shown undraped

or partially undraped was represented time and again. Then there were the nymphs, the bacchantes, and the other lively creatures who by tradition could not only go naked but could be sportive about the whole thing because, like Venus, they had been playing the culture circuit since ancient times.

Children were almost as popular as nudes, and it was even easier to find things for them to do. Without question, the Salon produced in its simpering, mincing pictures of childhood the most offensively coy images in the history of painting. Animals were often painted in much the same vein, self-consciously engaged in being cute. At other times they were reproduced objectively enough, going about their normal occupations of grazing or just standing still. Cows and sheep held an unreasonable fascination for Salon painters and their public, explainable, possibly, as urban man's nostalgic recollection of a more tranquil pastoral age. The cow in the living room became a familiar phenomenon, and a painter's knowledge of bovine anatomy was commented on as seriously as other painters' knowledge of the human figure.

Rosa Bonheur in France and Sir Edwin Landseer in England were the most conspicuous animal painters. Landseer could give a stag at eve all the pompous air of an eminent clubman, and his dogs were noted for their sensitive intelligence and subtle emotional responses. Landseer pushed his special variation of the pathetic fallacy to new limits; his animals ran an emotional gamut as wide as that of the French nudes. He was not so much a painter as he was the Sarah Bernhardt of taxidermy.

To categorize pictures of the Salon type, whether French, German, English, or of any other country, we would have to list the history pictures, the picturesque landscapes, the picturesque interiors, the travelogue pictures—usually of the Near East, the jolly peasants, the noble peasants, the pert old ladies, the melancholy old ladies, the fashionable portraits, the religious pictures, the allegories, and the imitations of every old master then in favor. One could belabor each of these types in turn, but in the end we would come down to the same conclusion: that the rank and file of Salon painting was skillfully trite, obvious, and vulgar.

So much for that. It is a harsh judgment, but now the usual one on a kind of painting that offers a field day for gibes. It is helpless in its awfulness, exposed in all its shortcomings, unpardonable in its sentimentality in a day when "sentimental" is a more damning word than "obscene." Yet, if Gérôme is ludicrous in *Pygmalion and Galatea* and in nine-tenths of the rest of his work, and merely dull in nine-tenths of the remaining fraction, occasionally he paints an anecdote like *Duel After the Masquerade* (page 68), which is so nicely patterned, so succinct in its narrative, and so unexpected in the nature of the narrative, that only a fanatic modernist can refuse to recognize its virtues. And if most Salon children are offensive brats, a few of them have great charm. Salon painting was based on a precise imitation of nature, in spite of all the prettying-up and the artificial posing. When children were painted directly, sympathetically, and without all the rigmarole that turned them into bad actors on amateur night, they could be attractive subjects for a kind of painting that was expert in the presentation of externals. And if Landseer's animals are usually mawkish, he also painted *Blackcock* (page 68), a harmony in whites, tans, and greys with a spot of red, in pigment so opulently weighted that the picture would do credit to Courbet. The good Landseers, isolated from the infection of the typical mass of his work, suggest that here was one of the best minor painters of his century, instead of one of the laughable worst.

There is gold in the storerooms; it need only be panned out. As a random example, there is the *Moorish Chief* by Eduard Charlemont (page 69), an Austrian who was born in 1848 and died in 1906, who apparently had a moderate success during his lifetime but whose name, surely, would not be familiar to one out of fifty or a hundred curators of painting or historians and teachers of art. There is not much reason why it should be. He was in no way an innovator, and he probably painted large numbers of dull pictures. But his *Moorish Chief*, which has been pulled out of storage in Philadelphia and is the kind of picture that might as easily have been found in a secondhand shop or in the random stock of an unselective dealer, is a beautiful piece of work, expertly painted, richly colored, superbly drawn, and neatly joined. These satisfactions are offered for themselves and can be enjoyed for themselves; the subject, a conventional bit of orientalism, is only a peg upon which to hang them and is unobtrusive because it is not forced into a pretense of more depth than it has.

Charlemont takes little more interest in his model as a Moorish chieftain than the cubists took in the violins, tables, and compotes that served them as points of departure for technical exercises. But his exercise is at least as legitimate, in many ways more difficult, and at the moment not a bit more threadbare, than exercises in abstraction; it is just that the abstract virtues of figurative painting are assumed not to exist by critics and artists who cannot see beyond their noses because these have for so long been pressed against nonfigurative canvases. It is easy to imagine Picasso or, even

more, Matisse responding to the merits of *Moorish Chief;* it is impossible to imagine the little Picassos and the little Matisses doing so, since they are committed to a blanket rejection of representational painting unless it bears the tag of a great name. With a falsified label (say, Delacroix, 1824), *Moorish Chief* would be sensational not only as an important picture historically, which it is not, but also as a superb piece of painting, which it is.

There are several good arguments in favor of ending the exile of Salon painting. The most objective one is that as part of the context of nineteenth-century art it has been neglected. Historians always weight the scale, but good ones do not pretend that certain things did not happen just because they don't approve of them. Regarding himself as an arbiter of taste, a museum curator of painting may decide for himself what he wants to hang (and lay himself wide open to the delighted laughter of the next generation); but regarding himself as the caretaker of man's long pictorial record of himself, the curator might try for a more representative display of that record than he has done recently in the case of nineteenth-century painting.

Outside the museums there are other reasons for lifting the ban. With Cézannes selling for half a million (which is not too much for a Cézanne, but is more than most of us can afford) and *Moorish Chief* selling for a few hundred dollars, the delight of owning a good painting is likely to lead collectors (and dealers) into new fields. In addition, that good old Pendulum of Time (a fine title for a Salon allegory) is still swinging, and a reversion to realism away from abstraction, prophesied by some critics wishfully and by others fearfully, may lead to new sympathies.

But if the revival really gets under way, it could snowball for a reason that not many people can accept without dismay: Salon painting still appeals to a large section of the public for exactly the same reasons, alas, that it appealed a hundred years ago when it was fresh off the easels.

John Canaday, who last year was appointed art editor of The New York Times, *is the author of the* Metropolitan Seminars in Art *and* Mainstreams of Modern Art.

A Portfolio of Salon Art

Salon art—whether of the French Salon proper or of its English, European, and American equivalents—depended on tested recipes, and each popular Salon artist, like each popular restaurant, had his specialty. A combination of exotic locale and romantic anecdote was one of the basic dishes, to which the painter added his favorite sauce. A successful formula placed desirable young women in difficulties that were stimulating to the imagination, as in *the* Alhambra Interior *(opposite page) by José Villegas, which allowed the Salon visitor to participate vicariously in the maiden's fate without seriously compromising his respectable position as an art lover.*

The High-Class Cultural Nude

F rench Salon painting was permeated by the national sport of l'amour in thin disguise. Adolphe William Bouguereau, the slickest technician of his day, made the worst of a good thing by reducing the noble tradition of the nude to barroom level. Typical is his Les Oréades *(opposite), but with equal aplomb he could paint a glib madonna. For more conservative customers, a specious innocence, as in Pierre Auguste Cot's* The Storm *(above), painted in 1880, offered less blatant titillations.*

Childhood and the Pain and Beauty of it All

*A*bstract aesthetic values were beyond the Salon public. A picture had to be a picture of something, and preferably it should tell a story. Human interest slopped over worst in pictures of children being cute (Henri Schlesinger's Alone in the Studio, opposite) and of popular storybook characters in moments of pathos (Randolph Rogers's Nydia, the Blind Girl of Pompeii, right). Essentially this art appealed to the vanity of the observer: it assured him of his cultivation and of the depth of his human understanding. As a variation on these formulas, Sir Edwin Landseer (The Old Shepherd's Chief Mourner, below) indulged a pictorial exaggeration of the pathetic fallacy: his animals experienced the gamut of human emotions. His faithful dogs, dignified stags, and long-suffering horses delighted Victorian England, and brought him international fame and a knighthood.

The Ubiquitous Anecdote

*S*tory-telling pictures ranged from guaranteed cultural situations like Sir
Lawrence Alma-Tadema's A Reading from Homer *(above)* through rustic genre,
as in Ferdinand Waldmüller's still charming The Picture Box Man *(below),* to
such laborious comedy as The Startled Confessor *(opposite)* by Jehan Georges
Vibert, who made a career of painting clerics caught off guard by the facts of life.

Frith: A Victorian Favorite

From the sticky morass of international Salon art a few names are beginning to emerge with credit in the re-evaluation of a century's taste. William Powell Frith (1819–1909) ran through a sensational career contemptuous of his arty contemporaries, the Pre-Raphaelites. At the big exhibitions his pictures had to be protected from enthusiastic crowds by ropes and guards. Enthusiasm

Now Making a Comeback

for Frith has not run that high for some time. But his panoramic Derby Day (1856–58) is a constant attraction in London's Tate Gallery, and lately a few critics have defended Frith's thickly populated record of Victorian life as an accurate social document executed by a superb technician whose virtues include the same loving observation of the world that flowered elsewhere in impressionism.

Exceptions and Surprises

Even the most tenacious academician occasionally lost his grip on mediocrity. The Landseer of The Old Shepherd's Chief Mourner *(page 63) also painted* Blackcock *(left), which can hold its own alongside of Courbet. While Gérôme's* Pygmalion and Galatea *(page 52) is a one-picture definition of corn, his less pretentious* Duel after the Masquerade *(below) goes beyond anecdote into fantasy. And an occasional painting by a forgotten artist, like Eduard Charlemont's* Moorish Chief *(opposite), hints of buried treasure in museum cellars.*

Life on the Educational Frontier

While the great debate continues in America over the state of public instruction of the young, some remarkable trails are being blazed by educators fired with what they regard as the "progressive" ideal. Every month, examples of their latest advances in the field of popular learning are assembled by the Council for Basic Education (a body itself not "progressive") and cited in its Bulletin for the enlightenment of fellow teachers and collectors of Americana. In order to make these known to a wider audience, HORIZON presents the following sampling from the Bulletin's recent pages:

Expanding the limits of knowledge: According to *Research Relating to Children,* a bulletin published by a bureau of the Department of Health, Education, and Welfare, a professor of psychology is preparing a study on the Relationship of Playing the Pinball Game to Personality Dimensions.

The enriched curriculum in California: School authorities of the Lake Tahoe Unified School District have specified skiing as a formal part of the curriculum for pupils from the first to the eighth grade. Yet in the more backward state of Arizona, the board of regents has recently disapproved the request of the president of the University of Arizona to inaugurate a course in bowling carrying academic credit.

More upgrading in California: The Fresno County Schools are conducting a Sunrise Semester TV series, described by the county superintendent as "a unique way in which school employees can join hands for mutual professional growth." Programs for October: Fundamentals of Touch Football, Fundamentals of Volleyball, How Big Is Space, and Fundamentals of Boys' Basketball.

Newsy notes from the world of higher scholarship: During 1957, Teachers College, Columbia University, accepted a dissertation for the degree of Doctor of Education entitled: "The organization and administration of college bands." Apparently the author did not exhaust the sum total of human knowledge on the subject, for during the same year there appeared another Teachers College dissertation bearing the challenging title, "The organization and development of bands in privately controlled colleges with student enrollment of less than 1,000 students."

More newsy notes from the world of higher scholarship (big muscle department): During 1957–58, candidates for the Ed.D. degree at Teachers College, Columbia University, submitted dissertations on the following subjects: "A study of physical education for girls in the senior high schools of Indiana"; "Sports officiating for men in schools and colleges with special implications for Ohio"; "The development of a functional approach to the teaching of sports in the preservice education of physical education major students at the University of North Carolina with special reference to football."

Facing up to the times: The sixth annual clinic for high school cheerleaders, which aims to "show the youngsters the art of crowd control, with a positive approach to cheering," has been held at the University of Alabama. The Barnstable, Massachusetts, high school gives a ten-week course in baby-sitting. High school students in Harbor Springs, Michigan, take an eight-day course in deer-hunting. Those who "pass" get two days off to hunt.

DRAWINGS BY RICHARD ERDOES

How to meet the Soviet challenge in education: A supplement to the syllabus in English published by the New York State Education Department suggests setting up a unit in the senior high school on how to use the telephone.

Culture via the cafeteria: A report of the recent annual meeting of the American School Food Service Association, published in *The Nation's Schools,* claims for the school lunch that it offers opportunity "to gain self-confidence in an eating situation." Apparently one result of this important meeting will be an attempt to prepare "a statement of the philosophy of school feeding."

HOW TO EAT LOBSTER

Matrimonial notes: As part of the widespread public school course in Home and Family Living, mock weddings seem to be here to stay. Recently the Hanover Park, New Jersey, high school held such a "wedding," complete with bride and groom, clergyman, parents, punch, and "miniature chicken-salad puffs." It is claimed that this fosters "better appreciation of the dignity of the wedding ceremony." Now Florida is introducing this custom at the fourth-grade level. According to the Miami *Herald,* members of that class at the South Hialeah elementary school recently held a night wedding in the school's "Cafetorium," with a cast of thirty-five. The bride's costume was "imported lace over slipper satin."

THE 5 BASIC BRA TYPES

Educational uplift department: According to the Detroit *Free Press,* more than 3,000 home economics teachers have accepted a Chicago manufacturer's offer of a free classroom kit, which includes a color film explaining "the five basic bra types, construction and quality features of bras and girdles," and "a record, teacher's guide, a companion student booklet, wallchart, and a demonstration bra."

A fresh stride in the liberal arts: An Associated Press dispatch states that San Francisco State College is about to offer a course called "Put Your Right Foot Forward." Students will be taught etiquette, proper dress, and how to write a letter.

ROAD SIDE VTILI ZATION ROUTE 66

Heirs of Aristotle: At Illinois State Normal University, a candidate has been granted the degree of Master of Science in Education for weighing the implications of this subject: "Roadside utilization along selected bypass sites U.S. Route 66 in Illinois."

What-will-they-think-of-next department: Mount San Antonio College, California, offers a course for credit called Hope Chest 61A and 61B, held at the college's modern practice home, where girls "can experience the various phases of home living," including instruction in the selection and upkeep of linen, silver, home appliances, and the planning of the wedding, the wedding party, and the trousseau. The same college also offers a course titled Modern Hostess 65A and 65B which includes, among other things, instruction in preparing quick luncheons, entertaining, and planning special menus for holidays.

NASHIONAL EDOOCATION WEAK

Earthy appeal: American Education Week in 1959 was marked on the radio by a one-minute public service radio announcement, sponsored by the National Education Association and spoken by a well-known hillbilly comedian, and described by the NEA as being "bright, light, and 'listenable.'" Sample excerpts: "You see now, this is American Education Week, and I say it behooves all of you outstandin' good folks to go see for yourselfs what' goin' on in your schools. . . . Are your young'uns learnin' all that good-lookin' arithmetic and geography they're supposed to know? Are they havin' fun in school? You'll get a lot out of visitin' your school, and so will your young'uns."

THE KING
OF INSTRUMENTS
RETURNS

America's leading organist describes the victory of a noble voice over technological "improvements"

By E. POWER BIGGS

Sometime in the last century, the organ—the favorite instrument of Bach, Handel, and Mozart, and in their view the king of them all—was toppled from its throne. When it lapsed from public favor, it lapsed from grace. It lost its aristocratic voice and manners, developed slovenly habits, and grew increasingly windy, pompous, and boring. Senility, one might say; after all, is it not among the oldest of living instruments? But old age had nothing to do with it. The organ's deterioration began with the arrival of modern technology (here, as elsewhere, not an unmixed blessing) and its application to organ building. The old instrument was, in fact, the victim of too many efforts to improve it.

But in recent years there has been a great change, an upsurge of interest in the organ at its royal, or pre-electrical, best. And this, paradoxically, has also been the result of technological advance. For organists are now able to go back over the centuries, so to speak, to find old instruments scattered in out-of-the-way places in Europe —some the very instruments on which such composers as Bach, Handel, Mozart, and others even earlier played—and to bring them back to life for a general public by means of recordings. As a result, many people are for the first time listening critically to organ tone.

Taking off for a concert trip, a flute player pops his instrument into his pocket. The violinist tucks his under his arm. Paderewski took his own piano in his private railroad car (although today serviceable recital instruments can be found in most major cities). Yet for the organist, any thought of taking his instrument with him is about as practical as moving the Rock of Gibraltar. You have to go to the organ—sometimes a matter of hundreds or even thousands of miles. For it by no means follows that the greater the metropolis, the better is the organ to be found there. I myself have crisscrossed Europe to seek out splendid old instruments in towns and remote villages from Iceland to the Tyrol and provincial Spain. Last year, for the recording of Handel's Sixteen Concertos for Organ and Orchestra, I was fortunate in locating an organ that the composer had not only played but had helped to design. I found it in the middle of the Forest of Arden, in the small parish church on the estate of the Earl of Aylesford at Great Packington in Warwickshire. By extraordinary good fortune this organ had survived two hundred and ten years in the condition that Handel himself played it. Not that it had been mute in the intervening centuries; but it had been, to say the least, inaccessible. (Electricity had never been supplied to the building in which the organ stands, so that it was necessary to have a power line laid across many fields and sheepfolds to run the recording equipment.)

But why go to so much trouble to ferret out the remote old organs of another age when there are so many newer, bigger, supposedly more efficient ones nearer at hand? You might think it an exercise in mere antiquarianism until you hear the differences between them. Not only are many of the veterans of two and even three or more

In this detail from a French tapestry woven about 1500, the lady plays a positive organ (a small, free-standing, portable type), while a servant pumps the bellows.

centuries still in prime playing condition, but they are unique in that they convey the exact sounds the composers heard when they wrote for them. Moreover, they are far better musical instruments than the huge electrically controlled behemoths you find in many tabernacles, concert and convention halls, and churches in our own day.

Consider the organs at Lüneburg, Lübeck, and Hamburg, once played by Johann Sebastian Bach. To hear the master's music on these warm and articulate instruments is almost to hear it for the first time. Consider, too, a name less generally associated with the organ—Wolfgang Amadeus Mozart. Mozart's letters to his family are full of references to his delight in playing different organs, and on one occasion he wrote to his father: "To my mind and ears, the organ is the king of all instruments." As a young man he even played the organ in the Thomaskirche in Leipzig, where Bach had been the cantor a few decades before. Doles, Bach's pupil who was now the cantor, was so moved that he declared Mozart to be the reincarnation of his great master.

A trip three years ago down the Mozart organ trail led me to such small German and Austrian towns as Kirchheimbolanden, Mörlenbach, Fügen, Ybbs, which no less than the greater Salzburg have never forgotten their share of Mozartiana and kept the instruments he loved alive. Going north, the oldest organ of all that I played on was in the little village of Oosthuizen in Holland. It dates from 1521, the year that Cortez conquered Mexico, and one year short of a century before the Pilgrims left from nearby Leyden for the New England shores. Holland is really the organ Eldorado: from A to Z, in Amsterdam, Alkmaar, Bolsward, Gouda, Haarlem, on through the alphabet to Utrecht, Zaandam and Zwolle, one finds magnificent examples of early organs, well cared for and appreciated, and—in fact—each the pride of the town.

Two, three, and even four hundred years old, as some of these organs are, one is impressed—upon playing them—by a feeling of their youthfulness. They have served great music these many years for the simple reason that they were built on sound artistic principles. Yet working within these principles, which define basic matters of construction and more subtle aspects of pipe voicing, builders achieved an amazing range of tonal variety. The mellow tones of early English organs match the music of Purcell and his contemporaries. The larger instruments of Holland and North Germany, bolder and more clearly focused in sound, coincide with the sturdy proclamation of the music of Buxtehude and Bach. The organs of South Germany and Austria, though equally fine, are better adapted to the slightly more easygoing counterpoint of Pachelbel. In Italy organs were mostly small, yet of an elegant sound. Spain and Portugal developed a style of organ all their own, stressing the imperious flare of trumpet stops in fanlike array—Trompeta Real and Trompa de Batalha—but omitting almost entirely any development of the pedals.

Through all these instruments, small and large, from different centuries and from builders scattered across Europe, runs a thread of identity of construction and voicing. In attempting some definition of these characteristics, it must be said at once that all this explanation represents no new discovery. Methods of seventeenth- and eighteenth-century design that account for tonal excellence have been ably expounded for more than fifty years by Albert Schweitzer and other authorities. Moreover, a few—a very few—builders in Europe never forgot them.

The organ's growth and longevity are rooted deep in history. It originated in the Panpipes of antiquity (as did the flute), and there were recognizable organs as long as two thousand years ago. The Emperor Nero was said to have been quite an expert player on the Hydraulus, an early form which gained stable air pressure from the weight of water. His affection for the instrument was considerable. The story goes that at a time of great political danger, facing an insurrection against him headed by Vindex, Nero whiled away a day of conference with his military advisers by playing for them on a new Hydraulus and explaining its construction, finally remarking that he would have it transferred to the theater—"Vindex permitting."

Roman mosaic depicts hydraulus and trumpet.

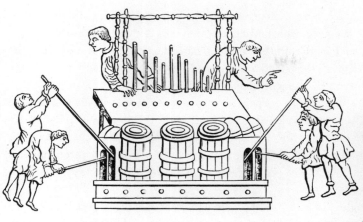

Above: The three water casks indicate that this double organ, illustrated in a twelfth-century manuscript, is a hydraulic model. It required four men to work the air pumps and two players —one of whom may have played the basic melody while the other supplied an accompanying voice. Right: The Bible mentions only King David's talent for the harp (I Samuel 16:23), but the thirteenth-century Rutland Psalter shows him seated at an up-to-date pneumatic organ. The man at the right treads a pair of alternating bellows; the one at lower left is playing a hurdy-gurdy.

Left: One of the most famous organists of the sixteenth century was Paul Hofhaimer, chief musician to Emperor Maximilian I at Innsbruck and Salzburg. This woodcut by Hans Burgkmair shows him playing a positive organ mounted in an ornate processional car. Below: Twenty bellows provided air pressure for the organ at Halberstadt, Germany, built in 1361 and described by Michael Praetorius in 1615. It took ten strong men, each standing on a pair, to pump them.

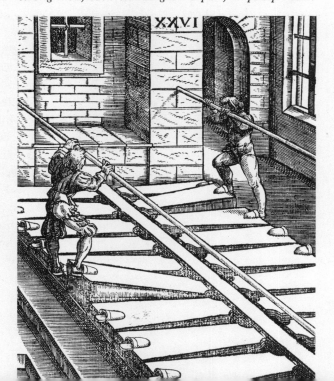

*Passage from Handel's
Organ Concerto No. 3.*

In medieval times, organs were exchanged as gifts between royalty. In the eighth century the Byzantine Emperor Constantine Copronymus V gave an instrument to King Pepin the Short, and in the ninth century Charlemagne received a similar gift from Byzantium. In view of these and other gifts, perhaps we should rename the "King of Instruments" the "Instrument of Kings."

Meanwhile, the organ, previously a "pagan" instrument, had been adopted by the Church and was steadily being developed in size and improved in ease of playing. By the tenth century, quite large instruments existed, such as the one at Winchester with no less than four hundred pipes. And by the year 1361, an organ with three manuals was constructed at Halberstadt. The pedal organ, to be played with the feet, was introduced shortly thereafter.

The violin dates roughly from 1500, the piano from about 1725, and the modern orchestra is a development of only about the past century and a half. But by the year 1415, when Henry V triumphed at Agincourt, the organ was a powerful instrument capable of producing "grandiose" sounds. It reached perfection by the time of Bach and Handel. The builders of the great baroque organs made their instruments more complex and gave them magnificent housing, but they never lost sight of their starting principles. Apart from their ornate cases, covered with decorative cherubim calling to seraphim, those organs were straightforward and functional, so that while baroque architecture may imply extreme elaboration, a baroque organ denotes simplicity. It was only much later, with the coming of electricity, that the musical identity of the organ became radically changed as its structure, voicing, and internal working were completely altered. In the process, its artistic purpose—the very reason for its existence —was forgotten. In effect the organ became (and still is, in most of our contemporary building) a great telegraphic switchboard, with the player clacking the keys and electricity and magnets operating the playing mechanism. The intimacy and sense of musical contact between player and pipes, so naturally afforded by the direct keyboard-to-pipe tracker action of the older instruments, were lost. Therewith went the organ's graciousness of articulation and tone. The sound lost nobility and became spongy and inarticulate. The bellowing cinema organ of recent times was the nadir— although musically harmless, since no real organ music was played on it anyway. Today's pipeless electronic instruments, though, are ersatz and worse.

By general agreement, the man who perhaps more than any other represents the high period of classic organ building was Arp Schnitger, son of an Oldenburg woodworker, who was born in 1648 in the village of Schmalenfleth on what is now the Dutch-German border. In the course of his long life, Arp Schnitger built one hundred and fifty organs on both sides of the Rhine. A Schnitger organ at Charlottenburg was to be the pride of Frederick the Great of Prussia, and another of his instruments helped interest Peter the Great of Russia in the art of music. Albert Schweitzer has remarked that "all things musical" focused in Johann Sebastian Bach; equally, Arp Schnitger, designing in his workshop in the little village of Neuenfelde, near Hamburg, is the focal point of the finest in Dutch and North German organ building, and many of his instruments were played by Bach.

Schnitger had critical ears, musical insight, the skill of his craft, and endless patience. But he had more. He knew and followed a set of principles concerning organ design and construction which had been evolved over hundreds of years. Just as surely as the understanding of weight distribution, thrust, and support enabled medieval architects to throw their Gothic arches to the sky, so a grasp of equivalent principles of pipe design and voicing, of wind chests and wind supply, of key and playing action, unfailingly guided men like Schnitger in the construction of their instruments. It is no fanciful figure of speech to say that the vertical up-rushing arches and spires of the Gothic builders is equaled in the tonal columns of the organ. And the exuberance of the baroque period that followed is reflected in their rich organ cases, as well as in the

This rear view of an eighteenth-century organ shows, with unusual clarity, the elaborate system of trackers needed to connect the keys and pedals with the various pipes.

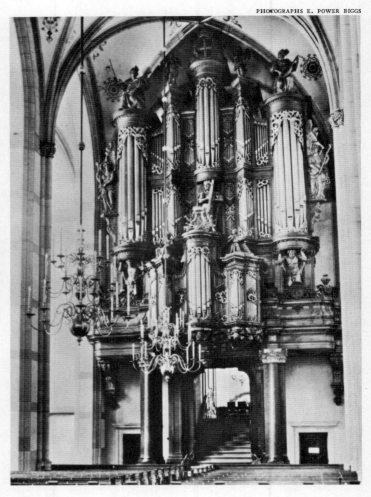

Upper left: Small organ, cast in 1557, in the New Cathedral at Salamanca, Spain. Above: Arp Schnitger's last organ, designed for St. Michael's Church in Zwolle, Holland, and completed by his sons in 1720—an instrument of incomparable sonority. Left: The new tracker-action organ, built by D. A. Flentrop, in the Busch-Reisinger Museum of Harvard University. Lower left: E. Power Biggs and Lord Guernsey with the Handel organ at Great Packington, England. Below: Mr. Biggs tries the biggest organ ever built—32,000 pipes!—in Atlantic City, N. J.

splendor of their sound. Buildings, instruments, and music went hand in hand.

As an illustration, consider Bach's organ Toccata in D minor. Play this work on the organ at Lüneburg, which Bach himself played and where the idea for the composition may have taken form in his mind. The three opening notes emerge with the authority of an arresting declaration. But the 32d-note rest that follows is no mere silence. It is made dramatic by the lingering suspension of the sound in the air, the tone receding gradually down the church. Then, before the echo has died away, in comes the continuing phrase, and so on, in an exciting alternation of musical statement and the suspension-in-air afforded by reverberation. The whole Toccata, a masterpiece of simplicity and shrewd writing, is inextricably bound up with the qualities offered by the instrument—alternation of manuals, contrast of registration, high pitch played against the low thunder of the pedals—and with the acoustical buoyancy and fascinating merging of sound into silence made possible by the building itself.

The conclusion is that there is one—and only one—way to build an organ, and that the excellence of the old is not a mere matter of luck, or antiquity, or acoustics. Most church and concert organs of today are not an "extension" of the old, as their apologists claim. There are basic disparities. Nor are fundamental differences in construction and voicing to be bridged by a few changes in present-day building habits. Not at all: the change must be complete, and literally must come from the inside out.

What are some essential characteristics of the old? There are half a dozen points of contrast between the old organs and our conventional modern ones: in the cut and voicing of the pipes that create the tone; in the design and working of the wind chests that supply air for the pipes; in the shape and movement of the valves that admit air to the pipes; in the pressure of the wind that activates the pipes; in the connections and sense of contact between pipe valves and keys at the console; and finally, in the actual placement of the organ in the room, auditorium, or church, and in whether or not the organ has a case.

Comparing the two, one finds, first, that the classic organ pipes were voiced to produce accent, or "chiff," at the beginning of their tone. Pipe tone had the essential characteristic of any other musical instrument, the ability to enunciate a musical phrase. Most modern organs are inarticulate in their tonal attack. Their tone is a spongy "AAH" while that of the older instruments is more of a "PAAH" or "CHAAH." It is largely through the presence and emphasis of these transient starting tones that a builder gives the organ its character. Moreover, since it is the beginning of a tone that commands attention, and since music is projected by a series of subtle accents, it is the lack of this "classic" voicing, and the consequent flabbiness of sound, that is so unsatisfactory in our modern organs.

Then, the old wind chest by its very design ensured complete unanimity in the speech of different pipes. The addition of electricity to the modern wind chest has disturbed this cohesion and altered, to their tonal detriment, the characteristics of wind flow to the pipes. Furthermore, the action of the older valves was more gentle in admitting air to the pipes. By comparison, the action of a modern valve is too abrupt, and the miniature blast of air which it emits tends to give the pipes a gulping quality. A low wind pressure produces a floating tone, a fact well known to the old builders but often disregarded by modern designers.

Connection between the keys and the air valves forms the nervous system of the organ. For centuries this connection was achieved by the simplest means imaginable —a system of direct mechanical linkage by wooden trackers. The many ingenious minds who have evolved the modern electric action have not begun to succeed in equaling the response and subtle inflection possible in the centuries-old tracker system. No player, having enjoyed the responsive touch of a good tracker organ, is content to go back to the comparatively dull response of even the best of electric actions. But electricity is welcome in an organ as a means of supplying air pressure, for it mat-

Carrying it too far

AERIAL ORGAN

Northwest Orient Airlines has installed an electric organ in one of its Stratocruisers, and beginning today passengers flying between Minneapolis-St. Paul, Milwaukee and New York City will make their way through the clouds trailing organ music. A Lowery organ, weighing 190 pounds, roughly the same as a healthy male passenger, has been fitted in place of four seats on the left side of the plane. The plane's public-address system speakers have been enlarged from five-inch to eight-inch speakers, the better to hear the music.

Six Twin Cities organists will take turns flying at the lofty keyboard of the might Lowery, playing half-hour programs with fifteen-minute intervals of silence.

ters not whether a rotary fan or human muscle at the bellows is the source of this.

Thus, the older organs not only have marvelous tone but also, if they are in adjustment, the most responsive action for saying something musically. Pipe speech seems to be right at the tip of one's fingers and is controllable to a surprising degree.

It is almost a new thought to assess an organ by its voicing and responsiveness rather than by the number and variety of its stops. Even though an organ is a gathering together of a multitude of wind instruments (i.e., the pipes) organized into ranks, or stops, it remains a keyboard instrument played by keyboard techniques. The coordination of keys, action, chests, pipes, and the articulation, beauty, and cohesion of tone are the measure of a "King of Instruments."

Finally, in the matter of placement, we have fallen into poor habits this past century. In older design, it was basic that the organ must be fully in the open within the room or church. That is, one should practically be able to walk around it, as around a piano. A chief reason for open placement was to allow mild and unforced pipe voicing. Moreover, the instrument must face and speak directly into the room, not from around a corner. A well-planned organ case is essential to define and project the different divisions of the instrument. It enables the pipes to "get hold" of the air more effectively. At the same time, the case serves somewhat as a sounding board, a function that is readily recognized by feeling through the touch its sympathetic vibration while the organ is being played. For all their ornateness, baroque cases did function precisely this way. They are hardly in vogue today, but the same musical benefits can be obtained in simple case designs.

It is in Holland today that one finds, perhaps, the clearest answer to the artistic challenge of the past. Modern organs of Holland, typified by those of D. A. Flentrop of Zaandam, translate the principles of the old into exciting reality for today. The new organ recently installed in the Busch-Reisinger Museum of Cambridge, Massachusetts (illustrated on page 78), is a recent importation from Zaandam. As one plays its sensitive tracker action and listens to the buoyant and articulate pipe speech, one senses the long arm of Arp Schnitger, the old renewed in the new, and one wonders how on earth musicians and builders ever came to gravitate away from such musical sounds.

To be sure, the genius of the organ is for the performance of polyphonic music. But whether that music be the exhilarating fabric of a Bach fugue, with its interweaving of many melodies, the softer voices of a simple chorale prelude, the romantic polyphony of Reubke, Rheinberger, Franck, or the writing of Hindemith and other modern composers, it will sound at its best in the musical terms of the classic organ. That a Stradivarius is excellent for the whole range of violin literature surprises no one. Hearing the best of romantic and modern compositions played in the slightly fastidious tones of the classic organ, one is no longer bemused by the idea that the organ needs a variety of essentially movie-house sounds under the guise of romantic voices. One is inevitably led to the realization that the classic organ is *the* organ—and the classic ideal is a unity, complete and self-sufficient. It is inevitable that the developing taste of players and listeners will cause such instruments to be constructed in America. Modern composers who deal with the same musical elements as did Bach and Handel, although in a different manner, will find the modern "true-classic" organ as powerful a medium for strong musical thought as did the earlier masters. Undoubtedly organ builders will discover that modern materials and techniques can afford improvements on the basic construction of the centuries. But principles of wind chests, pipe design, voicing, and playing action will remain the same as they were hundreds of years ago —a tribute to the generations of artist-craftsmen who perfected them.

E. Power Biggs has probably been heard by more people than any organist in history. Newest record: "Music for Organ and Brass" by Gabrieli and Frescobaldi (Columbia).

PILGRIM TO THE

HOLY MOUNT

ALMOST FIVE HUNDRED YEARS AGO
FRIAR FELIX FABRI SET OUT ON AN
ARDUOUS JOURNEY TO SINAI THAT
FEW UNDERTAKE EVEN TODAY—AND
LEFT BEHIND A LIVELY CHRONICLE
OF ADVENTURE BY SEA AND DESERT

This view of Venice, as it looked to Friar Felix Fabri on setting forth in 1483, was first published in an account entitled Peregrinatio in Terram Sanctam *by one of his traveling companions, Bernhard von Breydenbach. Unlike Fabri, Breydenbach was a poor writer; but he had the good sense to take with him the artist Erhard Reuwich, and his book is a treasure house of elegant woodcuts like those reproduced on these pages. Dominating Venice then, as they do today, were the Campanile, the Doge's palace, and— behind it—the domes of St. Mark's.*

O n a morning in April, 1483, the Black Friars of Ulm, in Swabia, stood at the gate of the convent saying good-bye to one of their fellows who was setting out upon pilgrimage.

Three years earlier Friar Felix Fabri, by birth a Switzer of Zurich, had gone to Jerusalem. Now he was off again, but this time to go farther and to brave new and unknown dangers. For he looked forward, on reaching Jerusalem for the second time, to finding other like-minded pilgrims there with whom to undertake a journey to Mount Sinai, the Holy Mount far in the desert, where Moses had received the Law.

As Friar Felix sat on his horse at the priory gate, the brothers crowded round him with last injunctions. They must all have read the account of his earlier pilgrimage that was to form the first part of his *Evagatorium* or "Wanderings"—his "little book" as he called it, which when finished would amount to two stout volumes. So now the friars detained him a moment longer as they insisted that in his travels he must once more notice carefully all he saw, must write it down, and bring it back for them to read. He promised, and he kept his promise. For, says he. "I never passed one single day . . . without writing some notes, not even

when I was at sea, in storms, or in the Holy Land; and in the desert I have frequently written as I sat upon an ass or a camel; or at night while others were asleep. . . ." It is from this travel diary, profuse, vivid, and humorous, that the following brief account of his pilgrimage is chiefly drawn.

The Friar and the rest of his party, a dozen German noblemen and their servants whom he joined at Sterzing, made their way thence to Venice, the greatest of all European commercial cities at this period and the chief port for pilgrims to the Holy Land. For the Signory, with its usual business acumen, ran, as a sideline of its merchant marine, a highly organized pilgrim—one might almost say tourist— service for those bound for Jerusalem. Summer was the favorite pilgrimage season, and every year soon after Ascension Day one or, more commonly, two big Venetian sailing galleys, fitted to accommodate pilgrims instead of merchandise, left Venice for the port of Jaffa, and returned after their passengers had spent a grueling fortnight visiting the Holy Places of Palestine.

So when Felix Fabri and his companions reached Venice they found, set up in front of St. Mark's Cathedral, two pilgrim banners—red cross on white ground—as a sign that

By H. F. M. PRESCOTT

the captains of the two galleys were prepared to accept bookings. At the foot of each banner stood servants of the two noble Venetians who, this year, were rivals for the pilgrims' trade: Augustine Contarini and Peter de Lando. These at once "invited the pilgrims to sail with their master, and they endeavored to lead the pilgrims, the one party to the galley of Augustine, the other to that of Peter; the one party praised Augustine and abused Peter, the other did the reverse." Nor did their publicity confine itself to words. Each galley captain invited the pilgrims aboard and regaled them with Cretan wine and sweetmeats from Alexandria, and both the promises and attentions of each were so evenly balanced that it was only the greater beam and, therefore, the greater stability of Lando's galley that tipped the scale in his favor.

Although both captains had been prodigal with assurances that the galleys were on the point of departure, Fabri and the other pilgrims found themselves condemned to spend a number of weeks and a corresponding sum of money before they could leave Venice. Neither was wasted. From their comfortable quarters "at the sign of the Flute," one of the hostels for pilgrims licensed by the Signory, Felix and his friends toured the sights of Venice, from the great Ascen-

siontide procession and the ceremony of the Espousal of the Sea, to a six-year-old elephant. "He keeps his head bowed like a pig, little eyes like a pig. . . . His nose is full six palms . . . long. . . . His nose he bends and raises, stretches it and turns it hither and thither; with his nose he does everything."

At last the pilgrims heard that the Signory, always jealous for the business reputation of Venice, had ordered the galley captains to delay no longer. The pilgrims made their last dispositions: they addressed themselves to Saints reputed to be peculiarly interested in travelers, took purges, and did their final shopping. This last was a matter of moment, for the accommodation provided by the galley was merely a space, one and a half feet wide for each man, chalked out on the deck of the compartment where the pilgrims slept, "a kind of hall . . . supported by columns." Although their contract with the captain provided for two meals a day, pilgrims discovered that often "feeble bread and feeble wine and stinking water" were what they got. And so, in addition to the mattress which the traveler could buy from "a man near St. Mark's" and sell back to him on his return—even if it were "broken or worn"—in addition to the sheets and pil-

Among the varied types that Fabri saw in the motley crowds of Jerusalem were (near right) pious Abyssinians—also called "Indians" with a fine disregard of geography; (center) Saracens, whose heavily veiled women with their boxlike headdresses looked to the pilgrims "like devils from hell"; and (far right) the ubiquitous Greeks who, according to Breydenbach, "infested" the city and controlled some of the holiest places.

lows, the coverlets and mats which the wealthy took with them, pilgrims were advised to take with them a barrel of water, a barrel of wine, flour, firewood, hams, cheeses, eggs, bread, and biscuit. Even a crate of poultry, with "a bushel of millet seed . . . for them," finds a place in one list.

On June 1, 1483, "very early before sunrise," Felix and his friends had the last of their stuff rowed out to the galley. On the next morning the captain came aboard, and as soon as it was light the ship was hung with silken banners; then, "with a fair wind which was blowing the banners up on high," to the sound of trumpets, the shouts of galley slaves, and the chanting of the pilgrims, the galley set sail.

Felix Fabri, with an inexhaustible appetite for experience that carried him through all hardships, found much to interest him on the voyage. The sailors taught him the meaning of the Venetian sea marks along the steep Dalmatian coast; he watched the pilots poring over the fine Venetian Portolano sea charts and learned from them signs of the weather "in the color of the sea, in the . . . movement of dolphins and flying fish, in the smoke of the fire, the smell of bilge water, the glittering of ropes and cables at night." Yet as the end of the voyage drew near, Fabri lost, he says, both appetite and sleep, so great was his eagerness for sight of the Holy Land, and he would sit waiting in the bows for hours before dawn, hoping that in the first minutes after sunrise he might catch a glimpse of the mountains of Israel silhouetted against the disk of the sun.

Jaffa was the port of entry for pilgrims. Here the rival galley captains were forced to come to an agreement before the Saracen officials would negotiate with them. While these settled the fees to be paid for registration and for access to the Holy Places, the subjects of their debate were herded into a foul, ill-smelling cave, there to suffer much annoyance from the aggressive impudence of naughty Moslem boys.

At last they were let out. It was dark, and the torches or glass lamps round the Saracen emirs' tents gave the only light as each pilgrim was subjected to the piercing scrutiny of the Moslem officials, and his name checked off in the registration book. He was then passed on, to be fought over by a crowd of country people who had converged upon Jaffa bringing with them far more donkeys for the journey to Jerusalem than the total number of pilgrims. On his first arrival Felix had endured this daunting experience and had been literally run off with by a Saracen "with a very cruel look." Yet the man had proved so kind and friendly that this time Felix had brought him a present—a pair of German stirrups—and when the two men found each other in the crowd "he ran to kiss me . . . with a most joyful countenance, and he laughed and said much to me that I did not understand."

After a day spent at Ramle and a night on a stony hillside under the stars, the pilgrims got their first sight of Jerusalem suddenly, "like a flash of lightning." They entered the city by the Fish Gate, now the Jaffa Gate, going two by two, in silent and reverent procession, all on foot, and some barefoot, down a long street. At last they were halted outside "a great closed church before which was a fair large courtyard paved with polished marbles of exceeding whiteness." One of the Franciscan guides told them that this was the Church of the Holy Sepulcher, for Christians the most venerated shrine in the world.

They began the set program of sight-seeing next morning. It was indeed "no light task." For ten days or so they had to endure "the intense heat of the sun, the walking from place to place, kneeling and prostration; above all . . . the strain which everyone puts on himself to earnest piety. . . ." Felix concludes that "to struggle after mental abstraction whilst bodily walking from place to place, is exceedingly toilsome."

The actual quantity of sight-seeing and devotion crammed into the short period was immense. In Jerusalem itself almost every incident in the Old and New Testaments had its traditional exact locality: the houses of Caiaphas, of Dives, of Lazarus, of Saint Veronica were pointed out; even the pillar

upon which the crowing cock of Good Friday morning stood was shown to the pilgrims. Round about the city there were expeditions to the valley of Jehoshaphat, the Mount of Olives, Bethany, and other sites. Farther off lay Bethlehem, Jericho, Jordan, the Dead Sea, and the Mount of Fasting, all of which were on the pilgrims' list. No wonder that, toward the end, on their visit to the Jordan, discipline and pious sobriety were cast aside. In vain the Saracen guides tried to bring the merrily bathing pilgrims out of the water. The devout Felix himself committed the ecclesiastical impropriety of swimming about in his underwear. Even religious recollection was tinged with frivolity as the pilgrims, "bobbing up and down, washing and cooling themselves . . . jestingly baptized one another."

In addition to their daytime exertions, all pilgrims were expected to spend three nights in the Church of the Holy Sepulcher, whose walls contained a multiplicity of objects of the greatest solemnity. In chanting procession and with lighted candles they moved from the Chapel of the Virgin to the marble-encrusted Chapel of Calvary, and from Calvary to the Chapel of the Sepulcher itself with its tiny cave-chamber, blackened by the light of many lamps. But alas for human nature! There was jealousy among them because rich pilgrims had bought "candles twisted and decorated with gilding and painting, and looked with scorn on those who carried plain candles," while some of the priests, in their eagerness to celebrate Mass upon the Tomb itself, fought among themselves for the vestments, to the great scandal of their lay companions.

But the long hours in the church could not be spent in procession and service alone, and for considerable periods the visitors were free to occupy themselves as they chose. Every pilgrim was eager to thrust his head into the fissure in the Rock of Calvary beside the socket hole of the Cross; Friar Felix himself, a tireless investigator, narrowly examined the interior of the Sepulcher and believed that in one spot he "discerned the naked rock of the original tomb."

Other pilgrims passed the time in far less elevated pursuits. Some slept or ate or "sat down together swilling . . . till the bottles were empty." There were other secular attractions besides food and drink: merchants who had paid a heavy fee for the privilege of entering with the pilgrims spread out their wares on the marble pavement—"not only Pater Noster beads and precious stones but also cloths of camlet, of damask, and of silk"—and noblemen of Germany haggled for bargains in a manner which Felix thought to be at once irreverent and undignified.

On the morning after their third vigil in the church, all but a score of the great company of two hundred pilgrims left Jerusalem for Jaffa and the galleys waiting to take them home. Those who remained, and Friar Felix was among them, were the stout of heart who had determined on the Sinai pilgrimage. Few of the several hundred pilgrims who annually made the journey to the Holy Places in Jerusalem had the courage or stamina to go on to visit the mountain; when Felix had experienced both and could assess the labor involved, he would rate the pilgrimage to Jerusalem, with all its discomfort, risk, and exhaustion, no more than "a holiday and diversion" compared with that to Sinai.

Having decided to go, they now had to wait till arrangements could be made for their transport, and for the guide to lead them across the desert to the Holy Mount. After visiting Sinai, still conducted by the official Saracen guide, a noble old Moslem of eighty, the caravan would continue its journey along the Red Sea coast to Egypt. At Alexandria the pilgrims would take their passage back to Venice in one or another of the Venetian merchant galleys, which in the autumn regularly repaired there for the great yearly spice market.

No less than three of these twenty daring pilgrims have left accounts of the journey. Those three are Felix himself; Paul Walther, a Franciscan as sour and self-centered as the Dominican Felix was merry, eager, and friendly; and Bernhard of Breydenbach, a rich lay canon of Mainz, whose

A PILGRIM'S VIEW
OF THE HOLY PLACES

Erhard Reuwich made for Breydenbach's book a remarkably explicit panorama of the Holy Land, half of which is shown on these two pages and the remainder on the next two. It includes every place of interest or veneration from Damascus at the extreme left to Alexandria (overleaf) at the extreme right. The pilgrims themselves are seen disembarking from their galley (at bottom, opposite) at the port of Jaffa. Above and to the right of them, vastly out of scale, is about half of the city of Jerusalem. The rest of it is overleaf, where the most imposing monument is the octagonal Mosque of Omar, or Dome of the Rock—built on the site of Solomon's temple, a spot sacred to Moslem, Jew, and Christian alike. Behind it and to the right is the Church of the Holy Sepulcher, a blue-domed tower marked with a double cross. Far to the right, in jumbled perspective, are Mount Sinai and the Monastery of Saint Catherine, the Red Sea (with Mecca on its shore!), Cairo, and Alexandria.

wealth enabled him on his return home to pay a "ghost" to write his lifeless and borrowed narrative. With better judgment, Breydenbach took with him an artist who supplied the handsome volume with vivacious illustrations (several of them shown on these pages) and who possibly undertook the printing of it as well.

The pilgrims left Jerusalem at the end of August. They rode upon donkeys, as they had during their expeditions in the Holy Land, but now were accompanied by twenty-two camels which carried, in the great panniers on either side of their humps, provisions for the whole caravan and the enormous conglomeration of the pilgrims' own luggage, the magnitude of which amazed even its owners when they saw it stacked for loading outside the Franciscan House at Jerusalem.

From Jerusalem to Gaza, and two days beyond, they moved still within sight of cultivation and human habitation. But then they left the last village behind them and came to a land where "there was only sandy soil burnt up by the great heat of the sun"; by noon of the next day they reached the desert itself, "the region . . . of immense desolation in which certainly no man lived nor could live."

At once the routine of desert travel clamped itself down upon them. Long before dawn they would be roused from sleep to begin the day's march. The breaking of camp and the loading of the camels was achieved, but only after a tempestuous scene; not only must every camel carry an equal load and each of the panniers weigh equally with the other, but the camelmen made each day's loading an occasion for blackmailing their employers. "They would carefully leave behind something, a bed or a basket or a sack . . . so that the pilgrim to whom . . . [it] belonged should be obliged to ask them to pick it up," and that of course would be done only at a price. Morning after morning the pilgrims would rage at the rascals, "but as we swore in German at them, and they shouted in Arabic at us, neither they nor we could understand the other." In fact, the travelers were reduced to such a state of fury that, as Felix remarks, "we could have eaten them alive, as the saying is."

After the noise and tumult of the start, the caravan would move off, silent except for the strange chant by which the camelmen encouraged their beasts in the hush of the desert.

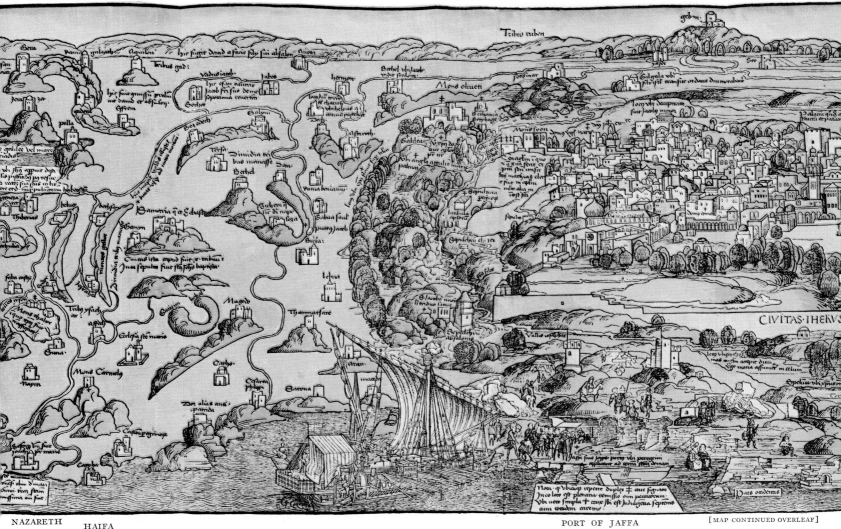

At first in piercing cold, and after dawn in pitiless heat, they continued on their way. There could be no midday halt, for the habits of camels forbade it, so that each man must eat as he rode such cold cooked salt meat, cheese, hard-boiled eggs, and biscuits as he could carry in the basket hung from his donkey's saddle, washing them down with the bottle of tepid wine and water which had jogged at his knee through the scorching hours of the morning.

Sometime before sunset they would halt for the night. While the donkeymen went off to fetch water and the camels were unloaded, the pilgrims had their own domestic duty. All, without exception, had to hunt firewood for the night's cooking; "ordained priests, counts, barons, and knights rushed about the plain," pulling up from the parched soil the dry and prickly bushes which in burning gave a sweetly aromatic perfume.

When supper had been prepared and eaten, and the next day's picnic lunch made ready, there was an interval of relaxation during which Felix sometimes explored the nearby desert and always made a point of questioning the old Saracen guide and the camelmen as to the names of the wadies and hills through which the march had led them during the day. All this information, together with the events of the day, he recorded upon his wax tablets and later transferred to paper, producing such recognizable versions of the strange Arabic names that the pilgrims' route can even today be plotted by a traveler who knows the ground.

Not long after sunset the whole caravan would settle down for the night, the pilgrims in their tents in the center, with their baggage about them; the servants and the tethered beasts beyond, with a no man's land between. The fires had been scattered and every spark trodden out so that no gleam could betray the position of the camp. Through the dark hours one of the pilgrims kept watch, not only, or indeed chiefly, against possible Arab attack, but against the certain marauding of the thievish servants. "Yet," Felix laments, "however well we watched, in the morning we would find holes made in the sacks, or eggs stolen from the baskets."

A little more than twenty years later, the desert journey was made so dangerous by unruly Arab tribes that pilgrims found the risks too great to take. But now, in 1483, though their ancient Saracen guide carefully coached the pilgrims

87

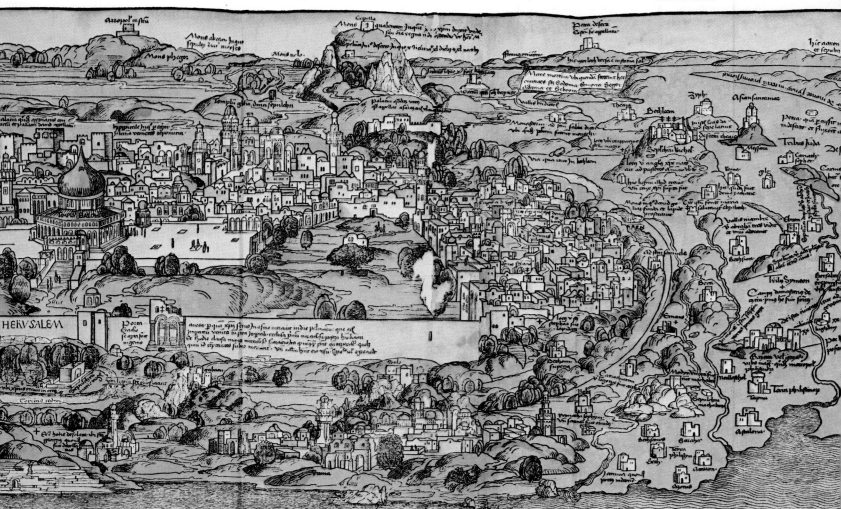

GOLDEN GATE

in the pacific deportment they should practice in any encounter, and though he consistently avoided camping near wells in order to avoid Arab bands, to Felix and his companions the Arabs showed themselves only as mendicants or, at worst, as greedy extractors of dues. Indeed, on one occasion when thirst forced the pilgrims to make for one of the water holes, after a few tense moments the Christians were so well received that, before the pilgrims moved on again, young German knights and Arab youths had competed amicably in running, leaping, and hurling stones.

Man, in fact, was not man's chief enemy in the desert: the worst perils were those of the desert itself. In one of the blinding sandstorms a man might part unknowingly from his companions and find himself alone and lost in the pitiless waste; if the storm blew for long, a whole caravan, unable to move, might die of thirst where it camped.

Heat and thirst, and the fatigue of arduous travel, even if not fatal, bore heavily on the traveler; none of Felix's companions succumbed in the desert, but one died on the return to Alexandria. Thirst was a day-long preoccupation, and when water was lacking the pilgrims longed with passion for it, even though it was dyed red and tasted of salt from the

waterskins or "whitish and thick" with a heavy sediment that made it look like milk. "We would," says Felix, "put our mouths to the empty skins, and think it delicious to suck the tainted water from the stinking leather."

Yet sometimes after such privations, and the more delicious because of them, there were interludes of rest and refreshment, as when at the bottom of a deep rock wadi the parched pilgrims found (as the Saracen guide had promised) water standing among the stones, pools where they might drink their fill and even bathe, green shrubs growing in the shade of overhanging rocks. "Never in this journey," Felix vowed, "did we enjoy ourselves as much as we did there."

Yet through it all, and in spite of the discomforts about which the pilgrims grumbled as persistently as God's Chosen People in this same desert long before, Felix found in the journey a strange delight. He discovered that for him the desert possessed an irresistible attraction, and since such an attraction needed to be explained, he attempted to do so. "It is principally this," he says, "that every day, indeed every hour, you come into new country, of a different nature, with different conditions of atmosphere and soil, with hills

CAIRO

ALEXANDRIA

had knelt at their first glimpse of Jerusalem weeks before.

Once they had made the descent and crossed the wide tract known as "the Sea of Sand" (Debbet-el-Ramla), which lay at the foot of the encampment, they were in a country very different from the desert through which they had passed since leaving Gaza. All around them were the magnificent defiles and peaks of the Sinai massif, fantastically colored with brown, myrtle green, purple, black, red, lilac, maroon, and crimson. They had left the utter sterility of the desert behind, and their hearts lifted at the sight of a shepherd with his flock. The scent of some flowering thorn trees seemed to Felix, fresh from the scentless desert air, the sweetest he had ever smelt. Best of all, they were able to gather from the young branches of tamarisk a gum that the pilgrims were sure was the very manna which had fed Israel in the desert. Canon Breydenbach, who rarely intrudes into the impersonal narrative of his book, here intervenes to remark that "it tasted sweet as honey and stuck to your teeth when you ate it."

It was not yet noon on September 20 when the pilgrims reached the monastery of Saint Catherine, a church and convent surrounded by the wall which Emperor Justinian had built; together with the monks' watered and fruitful garden, the monastery was set so close under one of the perpendicular rock faces of Mount Sinai that "when one stands in the monastery and looks upward it seems as if the mountains would fall on it."

Installed in the bare guest rooms of the monastery, where at this time pilgrims drew from the monks only firewood, and water from the deep, pure, and copious well within the walls, the travelers rested awhile before taking a look about them—at the church built by Justinian, at the little courts connected by small flights of steps, at the mud-built cells of the monks clinging "like swallows' nests" to the ancient fortifications.

They had to follow, during the few days of their stay, a prescribed routine of devout sight-seeing. Within the monastery, the church must be thoroughly and ceremonially visited. Without, the peaks of Jebel Musa (Mount Sinai) and Jebel Caterina (Saint Catherine's Mount) must be climbed.

The abbot and monks escorted the pilgrims on their visit to the church. There, where Justinian's mosaics were illumined by the light of scores of hanging lamps, the pilgrims, bearing lighted candles, followed the abbot in procession to the chapel where the bones of Saint Catherine lay in a marble sarcophagus. But by no means all the bones. The pious larceny of generations of pilgrims had left only a few ribs and leg bones, "a fairly big head without a jaw" crowned with a diadem, and the bones of the left hand, "white as milk . . . the fingers . . . long and covered with rings." When the pilgrims came close to drop their offerings into the coffin, Felix noted that the abbot kept watch with unceasing vigilance.

From Saint Catherine's Chapel they went—moving back,

of a different build and color, so that you are amazed at what you see and long for what you will see next. All the time something new comes along, which ravishes you with wonder, either the marvelous structure of the mountains, or the color of the ground, the variety of the rocks and pebbles . . . all of which delight the curious." Certainly this man would in any age have been a traveler.

Long before dawn on the tenth day of their journey from Gaza, the pilgrims set out by way of a ravine so narrow and deep that the moonlight shone only on the rocks far above them. By sunrise they had reached a high and bleak plain whose rocks and pebbles shone red, across which they had to toil against the force of a bitterly cold wind.

This plateau, however, came abruptly to an end as the ground fell away suddenly in a steep and rocky escarpment. For a moment this was all that they were aware of, but then they saw that the camel- and donkeymen were pointing into the great gulf of air which lay before them to the south. There, far away among a tremendous company of bare and jagged peaks, their guide showed them one "dark as it were with distance"—Mount Sinai, the object and end of their pilgrimage. Down went the pilgrims on their knees, as they

89

as it were, through many centuries—to the Chapel of the Bush, marble-encrusted and lamplit, where, stepping upon costly rugs, they reached the pavement before the altar, in which was set "a thin plate of copper, engraved with the similitude of the Burning Bush, and Moses sitting down taking off his shoes."

Two days were allowed for the ascent of the two mountain peaks. The start was made, as usual, some hours before dawn. Led by the sacristan of the monastery, the pilgrims climbed the same flight of stone steps and passed under the same archways by which the modern traveler makes the ascent of Mount Sinai. They halted at the various chapels to do honor to the Blessed Virgin, to the Prophets Elijah and Elisha, to Saint Marina; they also saw and wriggled into the "Clift in the Rock" in which Moses had hidden himself from the Glory of God. At the top they celebrated the august associations of the Mount with the suitable prayers and responses provided by their *Processionals*—little books produced for and carried by most pilgrims, which contained, in addition to these devotions, tourist information that Felix considered very inaccurate. Then they descended, but not by the way they had come, since the best approach to the stiffer climb up Saint Catherine's Mount was from the Monastery of the Forty Saints, a cell of the monks of Saint Catherine in the Wadi Leja. There they were to spend the night, and in the cool of the following morning make the second ascent.

But as they sat over the meal of dates, dried figs, and pure water that the monks brought to them in the delightful garden, where water from the rock above ran from pool to pool among the fruit trees—orange, fig, almond, apricot, pomegranate, and olive—someone suggested that those who felt equal to it should this very day make an impromptu dash up the peak.

At that, "ten hardy pilgrims," of whom Felix Fabri inevitably was one, "rose up ready to make the ascent . . . in the fiercest heat of the day." Halfway up, one of the knights found that he had overestimated his strength; sitting down on the blazing hot slope, he begged only to be left where he was. His companions first tried persuasion, then gentle compulsion; at last, with one hauling at a napkin tied to his belt, and two others pushing him from behind, they got him to the top. "A terrible business," says Felix, "we had with that pilgrim."

The official expedition up the mountain left the little monastery early the next morning by brilliant moonlight—which could not, however, penetrate the deep fissures in the mountain on which they must climb. And here, where yesterday the adventurous ten had sweltered and panted, the pilgrims were chilled by such an icy wind that when they halted, it was not, as yesterday, to slake their thirst at the two springs of water on the way but to light fires at which they might warm themselves. Even when they reached the top, and the sun rose, they could not "pray nor do anything proper" till another fire had been lighted; only when the

cold wind dropped were they able, first to attend to their devotions, then to look around at the superb spectacle that spread before them on every side, where the majestic confusion of mountain peaks and winding rocky valleys of the Sinai massif lay between two seas. Felix, at least, did not fail to remember that those seas were the highway for the ships that brought from India and the farthest fabled East "gold . . . garments of purple and perfumes, stones and ivory . . . balsam and outlandish birds, woods unknown in our forests, roots not native to all soils, from which for sick men and sound are extracted things medicinal and delicious."

When, after a merry meal on the small plateau of the mountaintop, the pilgrims began the descent, they knew that the turning point of their long journey had been reached and passed. They therefore took the steep rocky slope in holiday mood, "not walking but tumbling down, because we knew that we were beginning to go home."

Between that hilarious stampede and the actual homecoming, however, there lay for everyone except the youngest of them all, who was never to see his home again, months of hardship and anxiety. They would endure all the dangers and discomforts of another desert journey; they would have to submit to the extortions of Moslem officials as well as to blows and insults from the hooligans of Cairo. Seasickness, cold, and danger would be their lot in a prolonged and tempestuous winter voyage. And at last, in order to reach home, they would have to cross the Alps in the dead of winter.

And yet, once more, intermingled with all trials, Friar Felix found things to enjoy. The wonderful nightly illumination of Cairo brought him out on the roof of the pilgrims' lodging again and again to gaze and marvel. The chicken incubators of fifteenth-century Egypt and the vast mysterious monuments of its most ancient past, both were subjects for his insatiable interest. When foul winds held his ship in port at one or another of the Greek islands, he took the opportunity of making pleasant explorations ashore, storing in his memory views of the cliffs and capes of Greece, of wide seas and the narrow straits and small island cities of the Dalmatian coast.

Besides all this there were moments of vision that profoundly enriched and illuminated his mind. His experience and observation in Palestine and Egypt brought new life to his understanding of the Bible narrative. In Jerusalem he saw bundles of the dried prickly brushwood which is the common kindling for the countries of the eastern Mediterranean, and having seen, he decided that no strange and farfetched shrub, such as the books told of, was used for the

Crown of Thorns, but that the soldiers who mocked Christ had merely fetched the thorns from the kitchen. In Cairo too, as the pilgrims hung over a bridge watching a company of poor men mix the sticky Nile mud with straw, Friar Felix realized that just so had the Children of Israel fashioned their sun-baked bricks for Pharaoh.

But if as a priest he learned many things which must have added an incomparable vigor and liveliness to his sermons to the people at home, as a traveler he learned still more of the world that the merchants knew and of the great trade between East and West, upon which the dazzling civilization of Venice was founded—the trade which, in the form of jewels, rich and delicate materials, and spices, filtered through to the courts, castles, and kitchens of Germany.

From Saint Catherine's Mount he had seen the sea route by which the eastern cargoes came to Egypt. At Alexandria he saw the spices poured out in heaps upon the quay, and the harbor full of the galleys of western merchants who must buy here and, in buying, pay the preposterous customs duties which the Sultan extorted from western traders. That sight brought to his mind the sand-choked channel which he had seen near Suez, and he reflected how, if there had been "this way for the merchants of the world to trade everywhere," the ships of Christendom would have sailed to "the land of cinnamon and thence come to farthest India."

But Friar Felix did something more than merely witness the machinery of the great commerce. During the voyage back to Venice, he laid his mattress upon the enormous spice sacks in the galley's hold and found them a hard bedstead. In Venice, on his return, he stayed not at "The Flute" but with the German merchants in their *fondaco* on the Grand Canal, and it was with one of these same merchants that he crossed the Alps in January, over the icy roads. His own luggage—silken altar cloths from Jerusalem, baskets of pebbles from Palestine and the Red Sea shore, and palm leaves from Alexandria—was packed together with the spices and Murano glass which his companion was bringing to the marts of Germany.

In all this part of his experience the Friar was looking, as generation after generation before him had looked, toward the Orient as the source of wealth and wonder. But he stood at the end of a period. Less than a dozen years after Fabri's return from pilgrimage, Christopher Columbus broke through the Atlantic distances, revealed the new continent, and turned men's eyes and minds to new ways and to new and greater adventures.

But on the evening of January 29, 1484, Felix could have no inkling of this as he and his merchant-companion came "within sight of the sweet city of Ulm." They crossed the wooden "Sheep Bridge" together but parted at the gate of the Dominican priory in the southeast angle of the city, where only a wall separated them from the green waters of the Danube.

The convent gate was shut; the Friar could hear the voices

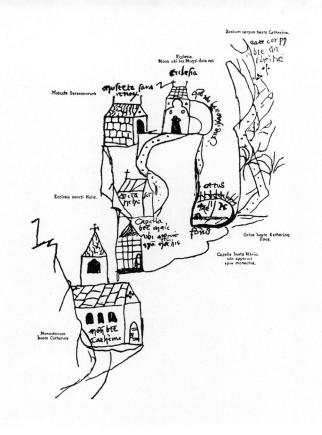

An earlier pilgrim, Jacques de Verona, sketched Mount Sinai's shrines in 1420.

of his brethren as they chanted Vespers; no one answered his knock. Or rather no man answered. "But I had hardly knocked for the first time when the convent dog was there, who knew me through the gate, and not with angry barking, but with a strange joyful howling and whining scratched and bit at the planks as though he would tear the gate down, in such a hurry he was to get out to me. . . . And when the gate was opened, before I could cross the threshold, the dog jumped up almost to my chest, rejoicing with extraordinary leaping and whimpering, and much tail-wagging; then off he rushed through the convent making a squeaking through his nose as if he were announcing the coming of his friend."

That was, says Felix, "the best welcome so far, from the best beast." But now the prior came running, "as if to put out a fire," and in a few moments all the brethren poured out of church, having got through Vespers as quickly as might be. They crowded round him, then led him in to kneel together before the altar and repeat the simple and touching prayers which gave thanks for a pilgrim's safe return.

Only when that was done did they all gather in the parlor, where Felix talked and, we may be sure, interminably talked. After his long wandering he had come home.

H. F. M. (for Hilda Frances Margaret) Prescott has written two books about Friar Felix Fabri's pilgrimages, Jerusalem Journey *and* Once to Sinai; *a biography of Mary Tudor; and four novels, one of which—*The Man on a Donkey—*was acclaimed as one of the finest historical novels of our day.*

OVERLEAF: THE TIMELESS STONES OF SINAI

THE
TIMELESS
STONES
OF
SINAI

The monastery of Saint Catherine (opposite) stands on the traditional site of the burning bush from which the Lord spoke to Moses (marked by plaque, below). It was founded by the Emperor Justinian in A.D. 527 and is the oldest existing Greek Orthodox monastery. Despite the ravages of time and earthquakes, probably few places in the world have changed so little. The dozen or so monks who now live there still worship in Justinian's own church. The collection of more than 2,000 ancient icons (upper left) is the greatest anywhere. From the monastery a path leads to the summit of Sinai (lower left), where Moses received the Law.

CIRCLE IN THE

In ten years it has become

the most famous

off-Broadway theater,

its record brilliant

with the stars it has launched,

its director's triumphs,

and the great plays

to which it has given their due

By ROBERT HATCH

SQUARE

The two founders of the Circle in the Square theater who continue to guide its destiny are Theodore Mann (left) and José Quintero.

A defunct night club at 5 Sheridan Square in Greenwich Village provided the makeshift premises for a group of players performing virtual theater-in-the-round: hence their name, Circle in the Square. Today their Circle is no longer in the Square, having been forced by threatened demolition to move to newer quarters in a ramshackle auditorium known as the Amato Opera on Bleecker Street farther south. Yet the name and identity of this hardy off-Broadway company persist. For ten years the Circle has been operating under the same auspices, headed by the director José Quintero and the producer Theodore Mann. And in the New York theater, ten years constitutes permanence.

Moreover, in an era when most theaters are controlled by real-estate companies, a house whose fortunes rest in the hands of the people who actually use its stage is a rare and invigorating phenomenon. The Circle does not dominate the theater world of its town as the Haymarket, the Drury Lane, or the Princess dominated the theater of nineteenth-century London. But something like that could very well be the dream in its proprietors' eyes, and meanwhile they have made it one of New York's most edifying fixtures.

Like all enterprises that sail into the teeth of wise advice to the contrary, the Circle has amassed a history lively with alarms and anecdotes. It has produced eighteen plays, four of which can be considered hits (though a hit off Broadway is by no means the bonanza that is understood by the term uptown). It was once closed for a year by the Fire Department and reopened (it is too bad, in a way, that another off-Broadway theater is called the Phoenix) only because Quintero and Mann found it unbearable being without their own theater. Then there was the Chinese youth who overheard a group of Circle actors talking of their theater's imminent collapse at the bar in Louie's next door, and who came by next morning to donate a thousand-dollar bill which he pulled from his watch pocket. He has not, it is thought, been around since, and his motive for the gift was enigmatic to the point of parodying the mysterious East.

When the Circle opened in 1950 with its first production, *Dark of the Moon* (a musical fantasy that was cheered by the critics and won four awards), it had no theater license and therefore could not charge admission. A hat was passed between acts, and the company, camping in dormitories upstairs, lived for weeks on communal spaghetti and other high-bulk, low-overhead dishes. In an early program, the management solicited playgoers for clothes, hats, shoes, and accessories to form the basis of a costume department.

The backgrounds of the theater's founders are interesting. Quintero, a native of Panama (he is presently the Panamanian consul in Jersey City, a relatively undemanding post that confers small diplomatic conveniences), came to this

95

country to study medicine at the University of California and became interested in the theater when he took a speech course to improve his English. Mann, having passed his New York bar examinations, decided to spend a summer managing a stock company in Woodstock, New York, and has not yet found time to accept a client. Roughly speaking, running a theater is a job half-creative and half-administrative, and from the beginning that is the way these two men have divided the work. Quintero is the director, Mann is the producer; they work harmoniously by respecting each other's areas of competence. The third member, present Circle management partner Leigh Connell, joined the team in 1955 as a script reader and today serves as talent scout and general artistic associate of Quintero. The plays that the Circle offers

reflect a Quintero-Mann-Connell judgment of how a contemporary theater should occupy and conduct itself.

If there is any pattern in the Circle's fortunes so far, it is one of predictable disaster evaded by unpredictable luck. The fact that its guiding spirits fell into the theater by accidental circumstances, which today even they can scarcely explain, may be pleasantly ironic, but is really a commonplace of such enterprises. And there is nothing in the record to explain why the Circle survived when most theater projects of a similar sort fail; it was no more carefully planned, professionally launched, or prudently managed. It survived essentially because its operators had a greater than average talent for the job.

What is important, and what does begin to define the na-

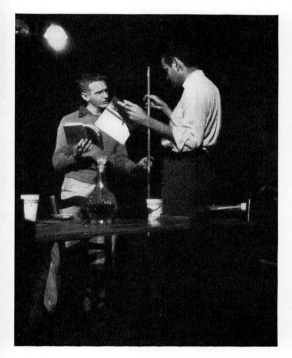

ture and significance of the Circle in the Square, is the fact that it should be thought of as having a history at all. Uptown in New York, theaters do not have histories, any more than hotel bedrooms have histories. They are efficient, highly specialized space for hire.

The Circle in the Square is neither efficient nor specialized. In its Sheridan Square period the theater had the form of a large rectangular room with low ceilings and a floor space cluttered by many supporting columns (some readers may remember the old premises when occupied by Greenwich Village Inn, one of the city's brassier centers of commercial Bohemia). The new Circle occupies a one-time movie house, long also the home of peripatetic operatic offerings.

In ten years the Circle has enjoyed four big successes:

The most salient contribution to the success of the Circle in the Square over the past ten years has been the artistry of José Quintero. The thirty-five-year-old Panamanian has directed all of the Circle's productions and infused each of them with his mixture of electric vitality and somber restraint. These photographs by Gjon Mili, which show Quintero rehearsing Colleen Dewhurst and other members of the cast in Edwin Justus Mayer's Children of Darkness, *reveal him through a wide spectrum of his mercurial moods: illuminating a psychological detail with a gesture of his finger (opposite page); demonstrating a lovers' embrace; pausing with absorption to adjust the flowers in a vase while the cast pursues larger issues; hammering home a cadence with a broom handle; and, finally, slumping into coffee-soaked exhaustion.*

97

Tennessee Williams's *Summer and Smoke*, Alfred Hayes's *The Girl on the Via Flaminia*, Eugene O'Neill's *The Iceman Cometh*, and most recently Thornton Wilder's *Our Town*. Of the Circle's other productions, approximately half were acknowledged to be artistic successes. But all the plays were selected and produced by men for whom the theater is a profession and not, as it frequently is on Broadway, a stimulating change from baccarat. The Circle is a "house" in the sense that a book publisher, an architectural office, or a law firm is a house—and in this sense no Broadway theater has been a house in living memory.

They have had flops—*American Gothic, The Cradle Song,* Francis Fergusson's experimental lyric play, *The King and the Duke*—but flops are not necessarily disasters from a spectator viewpoint. In fact, failure in the theater can sometimes be as engrossing as success; what is disastrous is the play that aims at a success not worth having (except in dollars). The latter kind is not staged at the Circle—or for that matter elsewhere off Broadway. There is no sense in selling your soul for subsistence wages, and subsistence is all anyone can make downtown and over on the East Side.

The emergence of the Circle (and with it the Phoenix, the Cherry Lane, the Theatre De Lys, and the Renata, among others) as a house with a reputation to build and guard has begun to effect the rehabilitation of New York's almost moribund theater audience. The theaters in the West Forties do not, for the most part, attract an audience; they attract a consuming public. These playgoers buy the prestige of

98

having seen a hit, and they care no more about what makes a play live than about what makes a Cadillac purr. They spend a lot of money (largely expense-account money) and they support a number of good plays along with the expensively packaged vacuities, but they do not qualify as a participating audience, and their nervous competition to buy success is one of the factors that has changed the Broadway theater from a profession to a fabulous slot machine.

No one goes to the theater off Broadway for reasons of swank. The surroundings are insufficiently sumptuous, big names are scarce, the plays are typically either classics or revivals of works that failed to hit the uptown jackpot. The only reason, in short, for sallying off to one of these outlandish addresses is the hunger to see a play. And as the idea

CONTINUED ON PAGE 119

Among the Circle in the Square's most successful productions have been plays that failed on Broadway. Of these, its outstanding achievement was Eugene O'Neill's The Iceman Cometh. *In this, Jason Robards, Jr., was catapulted to stardom for his performance as Hickey (above) the demoniac salesman. Among the Circle's other landmark productions have been Brendan Behan's* The Quare Fellow *(opposite, upper left), the first play by Ireland's convivial playwright to be done in the United States; Francis Fergusson's musical,* The King and the Duke *(opposite, upper right), which subsided after thirteen performances; Alfred Hayes's* The Girl on the Via Flaminia *(lower left); and Tennessee Williams's* Summer and Smoke, *in which the Circle triumphantly launched Geraldine Page toward stardom (lower right).*

EUROPE'S BRIEF FLOOD TIDE OF

PHILO-SEMITISM

Convinced that Armageddon was at hand, the God-fearing

Christians of the seventeenth century turned to embrace the

persecuted Jews—until the dream of millennium had faded

By H. R. TREVOR-ROPER

Anti-Semitism is a very old story. There is scarcely a recorded century in which the Jews have not been persecuted. A book could be written about their persecutions, and it would be a long and dismal one. I shall not write it. I propose to write a short and more cheerful essay on one brief period which saw the reverse: philo-Semitism, a movement of positive, disinterested cultivation, by gentiles, of the Jews.

Of course, since Pharaoh discovered the talents of Joseph, there has always been *interested* philo-Semitism. Throughout history rulers and landlords have constantly needed liquid cash and found themselves rich only in solid land and distant, uncollected revenues. The Jews, forbidden to own land or afraid to invest in a commodity which they could not carry with them on their next exodus, specialized in liquidity. So throughout the Middle Ages, Christian and Moslem rulers employed Jewish treasurers and financiers and protected them against pogroms. In thirteenth-century England the Jews were "the King's Jews." In fifteenth-century Spain they became the real aristocracy. If, in the end, they were expelled from both countries, that was because kings found it prudent to yield to popular pressure. But this philo-Semitism of economic interest, this love of kings for "King's Jews," is obviously quite different from the disinterested movement to which I now refer.

There is another kind of philo-Semitism which has also appeared from time to time. In times of jealous orthodoxy, of "closed societies," human thought has sometimes been liberated by "outsiders" who are free, or forced, to cross these heavily fortified intellectual frontiers. So in the Middle Ages it was Jews who conveyed Arabic science into Christian thought. It was Jews also—converted Jews who had never fallen under the full sway of Christian doctrine—who loosened the oppressive religion of Renaissance Spain. Continually, in such times, adventurous men trusted themselves to Jewish guides. But even this philo-Semitism, though more intellectual than that of Pharaoh, is not quite disinterested, and it is not with it that I am concerned.

The movement with which I am concerned occurred during one generation, roughly between 1630 and 1650, mainly, but not exclusively, in Protestant countries. It culminated in Oliver Cromwell's readmission of the Jews to England after an exile of 350 years. And it was not inspired by financial need or even by intellectual advantage: it sprang from a genuine, if somewhat crack-brained, cult of the Jews.

Of course there are always people who think that no movement is disinterested. There were people then, like Bishop Burnet and King Charles II, and there have been people since, like the German sociologist Werner Sombart, who suppose that Cromwell courted the Jews because he needed their financial support. But in fact this is simply untrue. We know all about the financiers of the English puritan republic, and there was not one Jew among them. Nor was the readmission of the Jews defended on such grounds at the time. In fact, economic reasons were advanced against, not for, their readmission: it was said that their rivalry would damage English merchants. The arguments used in their favor were religious, mystical, even messianic, the reflection of ideas which were not only English but European.

What was the source of those ideas? Scholars, examining the copious English philo-Semite literature of those days, have deduced their separate tributaries. There was the puritan study of the Old Testament, the new interest in Hebrew studies, the new belief in religious toleration. To all this we can readily agree. And yet does our agreement solve the problem? I think not. New movements are not caused merely by adding up current ideas but by some force which sweeps them together and along. In studying any movement we must always ask not only what were its elements, but what made them move. What force, what great event or experience, in those countries and in that generation, swept together and drove forward those hitherto quietly trickling streams? The experience, I believe, was the Thirty Years War, or rather the earlier part of it: the Protestant debacle of the 1620's (which was only arrested in the next decade by the miraculous appearance of a new savior, "the Lion of the North," Gustavus Adolphus). The streams which, in those tempestuous days, were churned together were the springs of millenary doctrine quietly bubbling in universities and parsonages throughout Europe.

All over Europe, and particularly Protestant Europe, for a whole generation, scholars and clergymen had been seeking to squeeze new truths out of the mysteries of the Bible, and to illustrate them by the new events both on earth and in the skies. By such methods they had already worked out the order of future events, identified the symbols of the Apocalypse, pinpointed the millennium, calculated the number of the Beast. The men who did this were often harmless armchair clergymen who nowadays would be sitting in their clubs solving crossword puzzles; others of them were distinguished scientists, mathematicians, educators. They certainly did not think they were launching a movement. They wrote in Latin, and often were not translated till after their death. Their ideas circulated quietly, often in a vulgarized form, in country houses and colleges, or were quoted with respect in pulpits. Then, suddenly, in the 1620's these academic prophecies assumed a grim topicality. The disasters which they had announced seemed at hand.

It surprises me that so much is written about the seventeenth century without reference to the emotional convulsion of the 1620's. Those years of economic depression and ideological war molded for life a whole generation, holding them together by the bond of a deep and terrible shared experience. It was comparable to our own experience in the 1930's and 1940's. Consider how the world appeared in those years to an impressionable young man in his early twenties, a man like Oliver Cromwell. He saw, all over Europe, the lights of Protestant Christendom going out. He saw his eastern allies

successively beaten down. He saw the apparently irresistible advance of the ideological enemy, Catholicism. From Gibraltar to Danzig, from Poland to the Channel ports, all resistance was overpowered, and the dull, harsh machinery of spiritual reconquest moved in.

In 1621 the Pope celebrated, by a solemn Mass in St. Peter's, the destruction of Bohemian Protestantism, the most ancient Protestantism in Europe. By 1629 the Huguenots had been driven from their last stronghold in France, the armies of Wallenstein stood victorious on the Baltic Sea, and the Emperor, by an arbitrary edict, restored to the Church of Rome all its losses in Germany for the last seventy-five years. Surely, Protestants thought, this was the Armageddon which Scripture had once darkly prophesied and scholarship now clearly deduced. Had not Thomas Brightman, the founder of the new "science" of prophecy, stated thirty years before that "there is an immeasurable gulf full of miseries already prepared, and that we do stand on the very brink of it"? The consolation was that Brightman had promised, after Armageddon, the millennium. By 1650, he wrote, the ultimate triumph of Christ would be made possible by that essential preliminary, the conversion of the Jews.

All through the early years of that great war, European Protestants saw the unfolding of the new cosmology. Every year brought new details to confirm it. And meanwhile its prophets were scattered and their doctrines more widely disseminated. In 1618 they had been concentrated in Prague. When Prague fell, many of them fled to the "Winter King" of Bohemia's other capital, Heidelberg. But then Heidelberg itself fell, and they fled to England, or North Germany, or Transylvania. But even there they did not feel safe. Wallenstein's long arm shook them out of the Baltic ports; Archbishop Laud scowled on them in England; in Transylvania, George Rakoczi was a precarious patron. As in 1940, Europe was full of displaced, fugitive intellectuals preaching, and sometimes revising, their "scientific" prophecies. There was Johann Heinrich Alstedt, "the standard-bearer of millenaries in our age," fleeing from Germany to Transylvania; there was his most famous pupil, John Amos Comenius, fleeing from Moravia to Poland; there was Samuel Hartlib fleeing from Poland to England; there was Paul Felgenhauer fleeing from Bohemia to Holland; there was Abraham von Frankenberg fleeing from Bavaria to Prussia. As they fled, they broadcast their doctrines, and their doctrines seemed, at the time, horribly plausible.

Moreover, as they fled, these men could not fail to discover another race of men who, like themselves, were both zealous and persecuted. In the merchant cities of the Baltic and the North Sea, in the ghettos of Eastern Europe, the

Protestant millenarists found fellow victims of persecution fumbling with like zeal through the same holy writ and discovering the similar promise of a Messiah. What the European Protestants, "the people of God," were experiencing in their own lives, the Jews, that other chosen people, had experienced throughout their whole history. Under the pressure of common beliefs and common disasters, a new bond was formed between Hebrews and Hebraists, cabalists and chiliasts. In the hour of despair many of them decided to pool their Scriptures and amalgamate their Messiahs. Out of this fusion under pressure and at high temperatures the mystical philo-Semitism of the European Protestants was born.

Of course, if one came down to details, there were plenty of difficulties. On each side there were solid doctrinal formations which would not melt in the new harmony. But what of that? The seventeenth century, the century of Pascal and Molina, of Jakob Böhme and George Fox, was a mystical century, and mysticism ignores or dissolves inconvenient facts. So the new harmonious stream swept past those obstinate boulders and the theological pedants who clung to them. A Christian and a Jewish millenarist found they had so much in common that they could, if sustained by wishful uplift, skip over the occasional differences. Both believed that the world was about to be convulsed, that the millennium was coming, and that a messianic savior would intervene. And anyway, in the end, the differences would be resolved by conversion. The Christians reckoned, before their millennium, on the conversion of the Jews, which Brightman had placed in 1650. The Jews pointed out that before *their* millennium the missing Ten Tribes of Israel had to be gathered in, and who could be sure who and where they were? Even so, the *Zohar*, the bible of the Jewish mystics, placed that event in 1648. The difference was very slight.

Thus Protestant philo-Semitism was a by-product of Protestant millenarism, and Protestant millenarism received its great impulse from the disasters of the Thirty Years War. Continental refugees brought that impulse to England. In 1627 the two most important books on the subject were published: one on the Continent, by J. H. Alstedt, the other in England, by a Cambridge clergyman, Joseph Mede. Both were in Latin, but both penetrated deeply into society. Alstedt incidentally prophesied that the year 1642 would be a turning point in the convulsion of Europe, heralding the millennium and the conversion of the Jews. When the year 1642 came and civil war broke out in England, this prophecy was remembered, and both Alstedt and Mede were translated into English. By this time it was not only scholars and clergy who held such views. A Kentish country gentleman

here, a Cornish country gentleman there took up the same cry. It was carried to America, and the Puritans of New England, by John Winthrop and Hugh Peter. And there was Oliver Cromwell, waiting "for the day to see union and right understanding between the godly people, Scots, English, Jews, Gentiles . . ." in other words, Protestants and Jews.

Meanwhile, on the Continent, the movement gained in volume. "The true light," declared the Silesian mystic Abraham von Frankenberg, then in Danzig, "will come from the Jews. Their time is now near. From day to day, from different lands, we shall hear of the miracles worked for them, and all the isles shall rejoice with them." Frankenberg, whose work was translated into English and dedicated to Cromwell's kinsman Oliver St. John, expected the millennium in 1655. Another and madder prophet was the Bohemian refugee Paul Felgenhauer. In his book, *The Glad Tidings of Israel,* he described himself as a Christian who, with the Jews, was awaiting the Messiah, and he told the Jews that the universal wars of Europe— the Thirty Years War, the English revolution—as well as the succession of comets which illustrated them, made everything clear. He, Felgenhauer, was the precursor (in accordance with this, he had named his son Israel and his daughter Jerusalem); the Last Days had begun; the end would come very soon with the Jews crossing the Euphrates for the conquest of their ancient home in the Holy Land.

An etching by Rembrandt of Menasseh ben Israel, 1636.

So far we have dealt only with Protestants, for it was they whom disaster had quickened into messianism. The Catholics in general had been at the winning end. But there was one Catholic country which had suffered almost as much as the Protestants of Bohemia and Germany and had responded like them. In 1580 Portugal had lost its dynasty and its freedom. It had become a Spanish kingdom and, as such, had taken the brunt of Spanish wars. In the East Indies and in Brazil the enemies of Spain, the Dutch "heretics," had destroyed the source of Portuguese wealth. Under the pressure of these disasters, the Catholics of Portugal, like the Protestants of Germany, had turned to mystical hopes. They too expected an earthly Messiah: their last native king would rise from the dead and bring in the millennium.

The most famous prophet of this movement was a Jesuit missionary, Antonio Vieira, one of the great writers of Portugal, whose faith had been exalted in the forests of Brazil. Vieira, like the Protestant millenarists, was steeped in the Old Testament prophecies. He believed that the Jews, who had been expelled from Portugal, should be recalled because he believed that they could re-create the wealth and greatness of Portugal. But his motives were not merely practical, for he also believed that the Jews could be converted, that the

Ten Tribes would be found in the Americas, and that, once converted, the chosen race would be the best of all Christians. In 1640 Portugal found a new hero-king, John IV, and began its war of independence. In 1649 Vieira persuaded him to found a Jewish company, exempt from the Inquisition and equipped with a fleet which would ultimately recover Brazil. In the same year he wrote his most messianic work, in which he prophesied that the new philo-Semite monarchy of Portugal would be the Biblical fifth universal monarchy, the realization of Nebuchadnezzar's dream.

So the Christians courted the Jews. But how did the Jews respond? At first, it must be admitted, they were chary. To them persecution was nothing new; they had never compromised with anyone in the past; the Scriptures were their Scriptures, which they were quite capable of interpreting for themselves. Why, they asked, should they reinterpret them for the sake of compromise just because a few Christians, for a change, were suffering instead of inflicting persecution? Of course it was gratifying to be courted at last, but what had these new allies to offer? In general, it was only too clear: the Christians expected amalgamation on their own terms, by the conversion of the Jews. As the aristocrats of persecution, the Jews were not impressed: they were not going to adjust their ancient attitudes for the sake of these excited parvenus. They would wait and see.

They waited, and what did they see? In Europe the great war dragged on. In England the revolution became more intense. Then, in 1648, the year in which the *Zohar* had prophesied the millennium, things began to happen. Peace returned at last to Germany. In England the revolution was completed by the trial and execution of King Charles, and the Puritan triumph launched a new spate of philo-Semite literature. But as European Protestantism emerged from its long trial, a terrible new persecution fell upon the Jews: a persecution remembered long afterwards as the worst they had suffered until the rise of Hitler. It was the pogroms launched by the revolt of the Greek Orthodox Cossacks against their Catholic overlords, the nobility and gentry of Poland.

For in seventeenth-century Poland, as in fifteenth-century Spain, the Jews were "King's Jews"—or rather, in that anarchical republic, noblemen's Jews. They collected rents and taxes, enforced seigniorial rights, controlled the economy, the life, even the religion of the great colonies in the south. And now the Cossacks of the south could bear it no longer. They had found a leader, Bogdan Chmielnicki, who told them how to strike at their distant noble masters. "The Poles," he said, "have delivered us as slaves to the cursed

Portrait engraving of Oliver Cromwell, 1652.

breed of the Jews." And so they struck at the Jews. For two years the pogroms raged, wholesale and merciless; and so from Poland yet another exodus began. The Polish rabbis appealed to the Jews of the Diaspora to receive the fugitives, and the Jews of the Diaspora remembered that although the crisis of Protestantism was past, the mood of philo-Semitism, which it had engendered, remained. Especially it remained in England. Could it perhaps be exploited?

At this moment the Jewish community in Europe contained a man both willing and able to exploit that formless mood. Menasseh ben Israel, a rabbi of Amsterdam, was a Portuguese Jew whose warm heart, uncritical zeal, and wide if shallow learning overflowed his own narrow community and functions. He had the gifts of a popular lecturer and spellbinder, and he sought a wider—that is, a Christian— audience. Moreover, from the Jewish side, he shared the enthusiasm of the Christian millenarists. He accepted the prophecies of the *Zohar* and the later cabalist effusions, so similar to theirs. He believed in the imminent recovery of the Lost Sheep (in his view, the missing Ten Tribes; in theirs, the obstinate two); and he expected, like them, the reconquest of the Holy Land. In fact, as they were Christian philo-Semites, he was a Jewish philo-Christian. As such, he wrote—he was the first Jewish scholar to do so—largely for Christians. His popular works were written in Latin or Spanish. His friends included the most distinguished Protestant scholars. They also included the philo-Semite Portuguese Jesuit, Antonio Vieira. By 1649 Menasseh had become the Jewish focus of Christian philo-Semitism. In the same year, under the stress of the disasters in Poland, he turned to exploit the mood which hitherto he had only reflected. In answer to the rhapsodies of the English puritans he wrote and published his book *The Hope of Israel.*

The purpose of this book was to open England to the persecuted Jews. His argument was that the last days were at hand, but that the millennium could not begin until the Jews could be said to be scattered over the whole earth, which must include England. The imminence of the last days was demonstrated by Menasseh's identification of the missing Ten Tribes, whom a Portuguese-Jewish traveler had discovered, just as Vieira had expected, in South America. For further effect, Menasseh dedicated his book, with protestations of complete personal disinterestedness, to the Parliament of England.

The English Commonwealth responded. Personal contacts were made, committees of Parliament appointed. In spite of interruptions and distractions—particularly the Anglo-Dutch war—proposals were made and considered. Menasseh was

CONTINUED ON PAGE 124

This is the third in the HORIZON series "THE ARTIST SPEAKS FOR HIMSELF" under the editorship of George Plimpton.

By KATHERINE KUH

"What is the point of soft without hard,

or weight without lightness?"

asks a sculptor-designer whose art,

like his own inheritance,

combines the traditions of West and East

An interview with ISAMU NOGUCHI

Isamu Noguchi is an artist of startling versatility. Best known as a sculptor, he has also designed experimental stage-sets for Martha Graham laid out the UNESCO gardens in Paris, and collaborated on the bridges of Hiroshima's Peace Park; his organic glass table and fragile lamps are familiar and distinguished household designs. Even as a sculptor, he is constantly searching for new solutions, experimenting with a variety of materials: stone, ceramic, slate, wood, bronze, aluminum, and plastics. His temporary studio on New York's 57th Street is a clutter of wood stacks, tools, models, and half-finished works competing for attention. There his latest sculpture— an unnamed effigy roughly hewn from three pieces of balsa wood—is set up unceremoniously in the kitchen, its power intensified by the accident of its setting. The studio is obviously temporary, for Noguchi stays nowhere long. Born in the United States of an American mother and a Japanese father, educated in Japan, Indiana, Paris, and New York, he has always been a nomad. Using Japan, New York, and Paris as focal points, he often sets off on trips to remote parts of the world. In personality, Noguchi seems to mirror his nomadic behavior; elusive, quizzical, remote, he moves and speaks

with quiet assurance. One senses almost immediately that for him mobility and personal freedom are more imperative than security.

INTERVIEWER: What made you the kind of artist you are?

NOGUCHI: Primarily, what we carry around with us is a memory of our childhood, back when each day held the magic of discovering the world. I was very fortunate to have spent my early childhood in Japan. I don't mean to belittle other places, but one is much more aware of nature in Japan—not a vast panorama of nature but its details: an insect, a leaf, a flower. Nature is very close, a foot away. Then later I came to America—at the age of thirteen, carrying a suitcase full of carpenter's tools on my way to high school in Indiana—and so I got the feeling of America superimposed on the old Japanese. It was a view of nature which was quite different. Here nature is appreciated for its vastness, its sweep, the panorama of that open Indiana countryside. . . .

INTERVIEWER: Were personal influences as important to you as environment apparently was?

NOGUCHI: My mother was probably my strongest influence. She was a Bryn Mawr graduate who was teaching English litera-

MARVIN LAZARUS

The nomadic Isamu Noguchi poses beside an unfinished work in his New York studio (above). A corner of his studio-home near Tokyo (facing page) reflects the fusion of elements in his inheritance. As Japanese peasants often do, he has hollowed out the earth for a studio, walling it off with thin board penetrated by a paper window; a niche holds an ancient Haniwa head. But as an American, he has placed indirect lighting behind his window and fashioned a simple ceramic flower holder that itself suggests a bit of both worlds.

ture in Japan. It was she who instilled in me a love of the artistic.

INTERVIEWER: How did you come to be a sculptor?

NOGUCHI: I remember that when I was about five years old I made a sculpture of a wave; it was much talked about in kindergarten and my mother never forgot it. She kept hoping I would eventually become an artist. When I was about ten she apprenticed me to a Japanese cabinetmaker who instilled in me a great feeling for materials and the use of tools—the use of the clean one-cut instead of the dirty two-cuts. This appreciation of materials and tools was further enhanced in my case by Brancusi, when I received a Guggenheim Fellowship in 1927 and went to Paris to work with him.

INTERVIEWER: What did you learn from him?

NOGUCHI: He had the same kind of love for material, the pristine, original, basic material. It was the wood itself and its contact with the chisel that he liked—not something faked up, painted, or ill-treated. With metal it wasn't some sort of patina he was after, or something applied with acids. He wanted to scrape away all the excrescences on the surface and get back to the original nudity of the metal itself—which for him was polished metal, of course. I too have a distrust of pictorial qualities in sculpture, of those eroded, decayed surfaces one associates with painting. What Brancusi does with a bird or the Japanese do with a garden is to take the essence of nature and distill it—just as a poet does. And that's what I'm interested in—the poetic translation. My father was a poet, you know.

INTERVIEWER: What do you mean by poetic translation?

NOGUCHI: To get to the kernel, to touch most poignantly the key forms.

INTERVIEWER: Could you explain what you mean in terms of something you've done—perhaps the ceramic *Centipede* at the Museum of Modern Art [illustrated at right]? Did you have a centipede in mind when you started?

The beauty of Japanese paper lanterns has inspired Noguchi to devise lamps based on them for Americans. In 1952 he made this colorful column from plastic panels as an experiment, now considers it "unsuccessful and trivial." But today his paper Akari lamps (page 111) are popular successes.

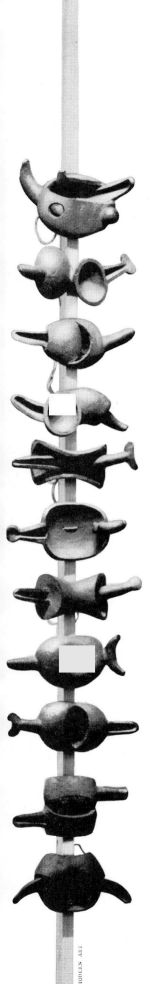

NOGUCHI: Yes. I was living in Japan then and our house there was filled with them. I became rather fond of them; I lost my fear. You know, when you kill a centipede, the two halves just walk off. This gave me the idea for a sculpture in sections —each a separate thing, though in actual fact the individual ceramics are tied on to a two-by-four. What happens is that your eye jumps from one image to the other and your subconscious supplies the connection. I also liked the rather quixotic notion of dignifying the centipede by making a sculpture of him—thus indicating that the centipede can aspire to humanity, or even to God. The work is a shrine to the centipede. Or rather the centipede is now enshrined at the Museum of Modern Art.

INTERVIEWER: To go back—did you always want to be an artist?

NOGUCHI: Well, at one point I was going to become a doctor, *faute de mieux*, because I didn't get on well with the first sculptor I was sent to work with. He was Gutzon Borglum, the artist who made those colossal heads on Mount Rushmore. He told me I'd never be a sculptor, and he put me to work cutting down trees. A friend advised me to be a doctor, it was safer. But when I followed this advice, I was told by Dr. Noguchi (the great bacteriologist, no relation at all), that medicine was not a science but an art and a very uncertain art at that—and one at which only a few people were gifted. He said it was much better to be an artist—more honest. He himself was an amateur painter—painted fish on his vacations—and he was very enthusiastic about my becoming a sculptor and really tried to promote it. In fact, he tried to get me to do a head of him; he offered me three hundred dollars. But I thought there wasn't enough dignity in his head; he looked comical with his little Charlie Chaplin mustache. Of course, he was a remarkable and great man . . . died, you know, during his work on yellow fever.

INTERVIEWER: And then came your work with Brancusi. What was that like?

Noguchi's Centipede *(left) is made of eleven ceramic pieces tied to a wooden post. His* Kouros *(right) is a structure of marble slabs in delicate balance. Noguchi says that it "defies gravity. . . . It's like life—you can lose it at any moment . . . you think, oh my God, it's going to go any minute."*

NOGUCHI: When I first worked with him, I spoke no French and he no English. We talked in gestures. He would demonstrate how to use a certain tool and then gesture to go ahead.

INTERVIEWER: What was his studio like then?

NOGUCHI: Marvelous! When I first worked with him, he had a magnificent studio—very large, made of brick. But then the floor caved in one day and he moved across the street to a temporary shack where he stayed the remaining thirty years of his life, some of it with those two white dogs he fed on lettuce and milk. He was patient and human in the early days; he hadn't become a god yet. One of the most important things I learned from him was the immediate value of the moment. I remember he used to say: "Never make things as studies to be thrown away. Never think you're going to be further along than you *are*—because you're as good as you ever will be at the *moment*. That which you *do* is the thing." But at the end of his life he was changed—impatient and bitter, as a god must be. I suppose old age and the incapacity to work, to express himself, was part of the trouble. He claimed he wasn't appreciated and that the few who did appreciate him lived in America and were connected with committees.

INTERVIEWER: What about Buckminster Fuller's influence? I've heard you speak of him often.

NOGUCHI: I met Bucky in 1928 or '29 and did a head of him. At that time he was working on his Dymaxion House. He thought all our ills stemmed from an accumulation of bad habits and weighty possessions—and that the good things had to be distilled back to essences. I think this corresponds to my own artistic outlook, and to my Japanese background. Talk of doing more with less—that's precisely what Bucky is after. I was saying to him the other day, "What's more fundamental than a pair of chopsticks?" What he's been trying to do is nail down one fundamental truth. In his Museum of Modern Art show you saw his *Tensegrity Mast*. There you have Brancusi's *Endless Column* in a new way. It's beautiful, especially at night when illuminated. Nothing touches it; it seems to float up all in tension.

INTERVIEWER: What was Brancusi working on when you were studying with him?

NOGUCHI: He'd done practically everything he's famous for—that is to say, rather than creating new forms, he was trying to perfect those he'd already done. He did many *Birds*, you know, more than twenty, I'm told, and many *Endless Columns*—always striving for perfection. He had a special feeling about things. I think perhaps he was a little extreme. The last time I saw him before his death he had a stainless steel circular disk (for his *Fish*) made in Germany. No one in Paris could do it properly. It came back machine-ground and polished, but he was quite unhappy with it and decided to do the whole thing over by hand. Of course, you do feel the perfection in his work. I personally wouldn't go so far. I'm a perfectionist too, of course, but not that much and in a different way.

INTERVIEWER: Are you talking about technique?

NOGUCHI: Not exactly. I'm always looking for a new solution. I'm not interested in producing things I've done before. I've heard it said I'm something of a technician, but I'm not, really. I'm more interested in *what* I'm expressing than how I express it. If I became too involved with how, the work would become separated from the fundamental question of art—which for me is the *meaning* of a thing, the evocative essence which moves us.

INTERVIEWER: But isn't meaning only revealed by execution?

NOGUCHI: That's true, too. You need technique to express what you have to say. But I'm afraid of technique getting in the way—that is to say, if you have too facile a technique, then you can express only those things which the technique permits you to express. You find yourself limited—to spiky forms, for example, or soft things. But what is the point of soft without hard, or weight without lightness? In Japan the philosophy of the relative value of things is carried so far that in ceremonial tea making there's a little cloth they use, which they handle as if it were the weightiest thing in the world. Light things are handled as if they're heavy, heavy things as if weightless—in which way one finds an almost complete control over nature instead of being dominated by it.

INTERVIEWER: What did you have in mind when you made the sculpture *Kouros* at the Metropolitan [page 107]?

NOGUCHI: At the time I was carving *Kouros* I was working with thin sheet material. First I started with metal, then wood, and later slate and marble. What I like about working with slate and stone is the quality of the material itself. A minimum of material is necessary, and you can use the space in between. The structure of *Kouros* defies gravity, defies time in a sense. The very fragility gives a thrill; the danger excites. It's like life—you can lose it at any moment . . . you think, oh my God, it's going to go any minute.

INTERVIEWER: Did you make sketches for it?

NOGUCHI: Yes. I made drawings and then models—in this case, paper models. You have to consider the weight of the material, the forces that conspire to hold up the figure—engineering problems, essentially. Everything I do has an element of engineering in it—particularly since I dislike gluing parts together or taking advantage of something that is not inherent in the material. I'm leery of welding or pasting. It implies taking an unfair advantage of nature. In *Kouros* there are no adhesives of any kind—only the stones holding themselves together.

INTERVIEWER: Does *Kouros* represent a human figure?

NOGUCHI: Yes. A purely cold abstraction doesn't interest me too much. Art has to have some kind of humanly touching and memorable quality. It has to recall something which moves a person—a recollection, a recognition of his own loneliness, or tragedy, or whatever is at the root of his recollection. In the case of *Kouros*, I was after the effigy of man. I've always been interested in Greek art, in which the image of *kouros*, the Apollonian figure, is one of the basic and standard forms.

INTERVIEWER: Why did you depart so far from the human figure?

NOGUCHI: It's the privilege of the artist to make his own translation, his own distillation of what moves him. I try to say what I *have* to say—in sculpture, not in words. I suppose what really moves me is trying to put down, to find my own image, in a search tied up with a lot of infantile memories. That *Humpty Dumpty* of mine in the Whitney Museum, for instance, and the *Centipede*. And other things that happen at night, somber things. I think of that table I made. I call it *Night Land* [page 110]. It's an image of people in bed.

INTERVIEWER: Really? I thought it was a landscape.

NOGUCHI: It is a landscape in the sense

The courtyard of the new UNESCO headquarters in Paris is the site of Noguchi's largest garden to date. He has used the traditional elements of the Japanese garden—rocks, water, gravel, a bridge, trees, and grass—for its design. The natural stones (left), which were brought from Japan, were arranged as sculptural groups by Noguchi to form the "bones" of his composition.

109

What appear to be megalithic monuments (above) are, in fact, Noguchi's Family Group *done for the new Connecticut General Life Insurance building near Hartford.* Night Land *(below), an earlier Noguchi work, is based on his "image of people in bed."*

that you can think of people as landscapes—a human landscape. Of course, there's bound to be much diversity in setting down your own image. There are many sides of me I want to express—the loneliness, the sadness, and then something about me which you might call precise and dry which I want to express as well. I wouldn't want to express only my serious side—I'm also playful sometimes—and then again completely introspective.

INTERVIEWER: Is there any relation between your moods and the materials you prefer?

NOGUCHI: I always work with whatever medium is at hand. I don't believe in sticking to one medium. I'm afraid of its dominating me and becoming my trademark. If I'm in a place where there's clay but no wood, I work with clay. I have no personal technical method or set of tools without which I cannot work; but, of course, I am influenced by the material to the extent that when I work in heavy granite, I become heavy in thought and emotion; I don't think of flying. Lately I've been considering a commission in Fort Worth, Texas. When I think of Texas I think of their water towers, and I'm inspired to make a sculpture of a series of globules of air or oil spouting from the earth, very tall and strangely shaped. I'd like to make them out of aluminum or stainless steel in the Convair factory out there.

INTERVIEWER: What about the UNESCO gardens in Paris [page 109]? Did the material which was used come from near the site?

NOGUCHI: Eighty-eight tons of rock were sent from Japan, all duty-free, but still enormously costly. They were paid for by subscription. Most of the rocks are natural —not carved—except, of course, for the four stone lanterns and the waterfall rock. Originally, I was only supposed to do a section called the Delegates' Patio, a triangular space too small for extensive planting, a sort of outdoor room. But when I got the Artistic Committee to agree to my proposal that a large sunken area next to it be incorporated, I was faced with a much bigger job than the means at hand allowed—at least if I was to make a really memorable garden. Specifically, I needed rocks, and I went to Japan to find them. The Japanese, you know, think of rocks as the bones of a garden—the plants simply come and go.

INTERVIEWER: Would you say the idea is

related to the *objet trouvé,* the so-called "found object" which plays so important a part in modern art?

NOGUCHI: The gardens are related to *objet trouvé* in the sense that there must be nothing ostentatious and self-assertive about them. It would do damage to the spirit of the whole for any element to be willfully apparent.

INTERVIEWER: You enjoy doing gardens?

NOGUCHI: Yes, I do. For me it's a highly sculptural affair, this three-dimensional arrangement of forms and shapes in a sculptural group. Contrary to most Japanese gardens, the UNESCO garden is intended to be walked in. The vista constantly changes and, everything being relative, things suddenly loom up in scale as others diminish. The real purpose of the garden may be this contemplation of the relative in space, time, and life.

INTERVIEWER: What about the bridges you made in Japan?

NOGUCHI: They came about, you might say, from a sense of guilt. As an American, and as a Japanese, too, returning there for the first time after the war, Hiroshima meant something to me. I had suggested doing a bell tower filled with bells from all over the world. Then Kenzo Tange, who was at that time doing one of the islands in the Peace Park, suggested that I design two approach bridges.

INTERVIEWER: Are they symbolic, the bridges?

NOGUCHI: Yes. The one that looks like a skeletal boat derives from the idea of the Egyptian boats for the dead—for departing, as we all must. The other, with its end round like a globe, or sun [at right], I call by the Japanese word "to live." Both were made of reinforced concrete, as is true of almost all postwar construction in Japan. The beautiful granite of Hiroshima was pulverized by the blast and only concrete endures —as if *that* is any consolation.

INTERVIEWER: Do you want to go back to Japan?

NOGUCHI: Of course I want to, but I would get lonely there. I would miss certain kinds of communication—the contact with other artists' thinking which encourages me to follow the sequence of my own thoughts. We all walk one step after another, you know. We all affect each other by supplying footsteps. To live permanently in Japan would ultimately be a hardship for me because I would lose communication

The dazzling chromium head of his friend Buckminster Fuller (above) was made in 1929. Noguchi believes that his Akari lamps (right) reflect architect Fuller's principle of lightness and essence, which infuses his bridge railing at Hiroshima (below).

with people of similar backgrounds to mine —that is, people like Martha Graham and Bucky Fuller.

INTERVIEWER: To what do you attribute the enormous influence the Orient has recently had on our art and our architecture?

NOGUCHI: In this country we appreciate doing more with less, and that is one of the appealing things about Japan—a compensation the Orient has given us for the opulence we have derived from Europe.

INTERVIEWER: In Japan has there been an equivalent interest in American art?

NOGUCHI: To the point where it's being imitated. Which is outlandish, of course. I mean if you *must* imitate, it's better to imitate yourself. Fortunately, we're so busy imitating the Japanese that when they imitate us they get a certain amount of their own artistic tradition *back*—twice removed, of course, like premasticated food, but at least they get it back.

INTERVIEWER: What about architects? I know that you have done considerable work for them. Do you prefer to work without the restrictions one would guess are imposed?

NOGUCHI: Though I'm not interested in making monuments, I have a certain love of scale in relation to man—which comes, of course, with architectural sculpture. But I prefer to be in complete control of the work, simply because the work, whatever its scale, must be relative to everything else . . . like the component parts of a symphony.

INTERVIEWER: Well then, do you do all your own carving?

NOGUCHI: Most of it—not all. Many sculptors knock themselves out. I refuse to become a slave either to a technique or a medium. Unhappily, I usually find out that I'm the only person who can make a thing the way I want it made. I don't do it because I want to; I do it because I *have* to. But if I could find some way of pushing buttons and getting the work done, I'd do it.

INTERVIEWER: Tell me about your portrait heads. Why have you lost interest in them?

NOGUCHI: Originally I was interested in portrait heads partly as a means of making a living. Then I got into the habit and kept on much longer than I should have. I don't think portrait heads are a complete sculptural expression. It's difficult to express what you want when you are mixed up with another personality—the sitter. After

a while, it all seemed to be nothing more than tour de force—whichever medium I used. At one time I made heads directly in wood with the sitters there in the studio and the chips flying all over the place; then when I started doing them in stone, I found that the type of translation was one I didn't like. Working in clay did not satisfy me.

INTERVIEWER: Why not?

NOGUCHI: Because in a medium like clay anything can be done, and I think that's dangerous. It's too fluid, too facile. For example, Rodin had a tremendous freedom of expression—he was actually an expressionist—but I wonder if it is the most sculptural sculpture. It's more like painting. The very freedom is a kind of anti-sculpture to me. When I work with a material like stone, I want it to look like stone. You can make clay look like anything—that's the danger.

INTERVIEWER: Do you feel that a work of art is ever finished?

NOGUCHI: It takes on its own life, and when it has, I feel it a desecration—a crime —to do anything further to it. If a work does not live, then I don't think anything I can do would help. I'd rather stop and start something new.

INTERVIEWER: Do you think that your own personal characteristics are evident in your work?

NOGUCHI: I don't think it is so necessary to be concerned with oneself. If you are continually polishing up your signature, it ends by being about all you do. That's why I'm against a too-conscious concern with style. I don't even like the idea of belonging to a movement. I admire certain abstract expressionist paintings, for example, but what I really don't approve of is their mass production.

INTERVIEWER: Do you find that your own work stems almost entirely from personal experience?

NOGUCHI: Yes, but not literally or specifically. In a sense, I feel the more one loses oneself, the more one *is* oneself. Work is something like having a conversation with oneself—not a commonplace talk, not "What did you eat today?" "Carrots!" nothing like that, but a personal soliloquy in which through argument and trial you try to nail something down—express the inexplicable. You can't tell quite what's going to happen when you start, but then *after* the work is done recognition comes: certain things affect you; and then you recognize that the work is really yourself.

INTERVIEWER: What kind of art do you admire?

NOGUCHI: Actually, the older it is, the more archaic and primitive, the better I like it. I don't know why, but perhaps it's simply because the repeated distillation of art brings you back to the primordial: the monoliths, the cave paintings, the scratchings, the shorthand by which the earliest people tried to indicate their sense of significance, and even further back until you get to the fundamental material itself.

INTERVIEWER: Which of the living sculptors do you admire?

NOGUCHI: It's easier to say whom I don't admire. I have admired Giacometti, his early work and sometimes his skeletal, isolated pins of existence. I enjoy his poetic quality. I think that he is seeking the poetic image.

INTERVIEWER: How about your own work? What are you working on now?

NOGUCHI: I've just finished something I like very much, though of course the latest thing one does is always the best. This time I started with the idea of man in a composition in which there is both the element of weight and complete lightness—the two together balancing each other.

INTERVIEWER: Is the material you use here heavy?

NOGUCHI: No, it's the shape that's heavy. I've carved it in balsa wood—one very heavy shape counterbalanced by the sheer lightness of the other.

INTERVIEWER: What is it called?

NOGUCHI: I haven't decided on a name.

INTERVIEWER: How will you finally decide upon one?

NOGUCHI: It speaks to me. I have a strong emotion about it; I can't tell you exactly what it is. I'm bad at names and don't pay much attention to them until the very end. The *Centipede* was an exception. I was dealing with a centipede from the beginning.

INTERVIEWER: What is it you're trying to express in this new work?

NOGUCHI: In this case I'm dealing with an emotion. On the one hand it's like a cry—on the other . . . well, you're asking me what I'm after. You're asking me to name myself. I can't. You must find it in my work.

_____

Katherine Kuh was, until recently, on the curatorial staff of Chicago's Art Institute; she is now art critic of the Saturday Review.

By GILBERT HIGHET

THE

proud, sensual, elegant, depraved, witty, illusionless

ALEXANDRIANS

of Lawrence Durrell

When *Justine* appeared, three years and three novels ago, most readers were fascinated but puzzled. Now, with *Clea*, the author completes his revelation of the minds and mysteries of a cast of characters hardly equaled since the Parisians of Marcel Proust

Turning its back upon Egypt, the city of Alexandria gazes over the Mediterranean Sea toward Greece and Italy. It was founded by the boldest of the Greek explorers and civilizing geniuses, the great Alexander. It soon became a mighty city, its magnificent library and university thronged by poets, scholars, and scientists; and for centuries it was second in the Western world only to Rome. Quick-witted, proud, sensual, hot-tempered, elegant, illusionless, the Alexandrians looked down on the people of other cities as half-witted boors. They would not be patronized, and they could scarcely be ruled. They mobbed Julius Caesar with venomous irreverence, and they taunted the brutal Emperor Caracalla until he filled their mouths with their own blood.

As they were in antiquity, so the Alexandrians are today. They are polyglots: educated men and women chat easily in three or four languages, and many more tongues are heard in the streets. They are sophisticated: for them, the Cairenes and up-country Egyptians are bumpkins, the folk of mainland Greece, of Syria and Turkey, naïve provincials. The superb library has gone, and the authors of ancient Alexandria are little read today, but the modern city has produced at least one brilliant and inimitable

113

DURRELL'S ALEXANDRIA:
NATIVE QUARTER

The narrow street was of baked and scented terra cotta, soft now from rain but not wet. Its whole length was lined with the coloured booths of prostitutes whose thrilling marble bodies were posed modestly each before her doll's house, as before a shrine. They sat on three-legged stools like oracles wearing coloured slippers, out in the open street. The originality of the lighting gave the whole scene the colours of deathless romance, for instead of being lit from above by electric light the whole street was lit by a series of stabbing carbide-lamps standing upon the ground: throwing thirsty, ravishing violet shadows upwards into the nooks and gables of the dolls' houses, into the nostrils and eyes of its inhabitants, into the unresisting softness of that furry darkness. I walked slowly among these extraordinary human blooms, reflecting that a city like a human being collects its predispositions, appetites and fears. It grows to maturity, utters its prophets, and declines into hebetude, old age or the loneliness which is worse than either. Unaware that their mother city was dying, the living still sat there in the open street, like caryatids supporting the darkness, the pains of futurity upon their very eyelids. . . .

Here was a painted booth entirely decorated by *fleur-de-lis* carefully and correctly drawn upon a peach-coloured ground in royal blue. At its door sat a giant bluish child of a negress, perhaps eighteen years of age, clad in a red flannel nightgown of a vaguely mission-house *allure*. She wore a crown of dazzling narcissus on her black woollen head. Her hands were gathered humbly in her lap—an apron full of chopped fingers. She resembled a heavenly black bunny sitting at the entrance of a burrow. Next door a woman fragile as a leaf, and next her one like a chemical formula rinsed out by anaemia and cigarette smoke. Everywhere on these brown flapping walls I saw the basic talisman of the country—imprint of a palm with outspread fingers, seeking to ward off the terrors which thronged the darkness outside the lighted town. . . .

The dolls' houses shivered and reeled for a second as the wind of the sea intruded, pressing upon loose fragments of cloth, unfastened partitions. One house lacked any backcloth whatever and staring through the door one caught a glimpse of a courtyard with a stunted palm-tree. By the light thrown out from a bucket of burning shavings three girls sat on stools, dressed in torn kimonos, talking in low tones and extending the tips of their fingers to the elf-light. They seemed as rapt, as remote as if they had been sitting around a camp fire on the steppes.

(In the back of my mind I could see the great banks of ice—snowdrifts in which Nessim's champagne bottles lay, gleaming bluish-green like aged carp in a familiar pond. And as if to restore my memory I smelt my sleeves for traces of Justine's perfume.)

Justine, 1957

poet, the melancholy sensualist Cavafy. They love vivid festivals: the carnival, a Moslem saint's day, a rich man's funeral, a circus, a riot. And they are boldly voluptuous. In every city of the world, most of the sensual satisfactions (so pitifully few in number) are available at the cost of some trouble and some money, but in Alexandria they are thrust upon you. The respectable old gentleman who addresses you in a café may take you to a house full of ten-year-old prostitutes. If you have money, the bellboy will bring you champagne, and if you look the type, he will offer you heroin too. An exquisite meal will be gracefully served by a handsome waiter who can himself be purchased as a pousse-café. Alexandria is a small Paris set on the central sea; but also, by tradition and infection, it is a city of the hot, intricate, corrupt Middle East.

Alexandria and its people have recently been described with dazzling clarity and suave finesse in four novels by the brilliant Anglo-Irish writer Lawrence Durrell. Before World War II, he was known to a few readers as an avant-garde poet. In 1957, in *Bitter Lemons*, he had some success with a sympathetic evocation of the once peaceful and more recently turbulent isle of Cyprus. In the same year, with his first Alexandrian novel, *Justine*, he struck a new note in modern fiction: passionate but disillusioned, richly sensual yet coolly intelligent, and there was something more, too—something like the perfume of decay, the faint rumors of collapse, the febrile anxiety of a civilization threatened by the oncoming barbarians. When *Balthazar* followed in 1958, Durrell's reputation grew. The third novel in the series, *Mountolive*, was widely read, and became the Book-of-the-Month Club selection for April, 1959.

This spring Durrell has published *Clea*, fourth and last of the series, thus completing one of the strangest and most poetic works of fiction in modern English. Each of the novels can be read alone—very much as the separate parts of Marcel Proust's panorama can be studied separately—but (like Proust's) they were planned together, and when they are read together, their impact, and the impact of Lawrence Durrell's curious personality and delicate art, is far stronger.

All four deal with the same group of characters, in their rapidly and dizzily varying relationships, and with the same city, at once lovable and hateful, sometimes repellent, always unforgettable. Each of the volumes is named after one important person who figures in it:

Justine, the dashing Jewess who marries a Coptic Christian millionaire;

Balthazar, the coldly intelligent doctor who observes and pities the passions of his friends while, as a homosexual, he can neither conquer nor ennoble his own desires;

Mountolive, the British diplomat who, until the final revelation, cannot believe that his friends might betray his trust in them;

Clea, the cool and aloof Frenchwoman, a painter who can love and be loved but who can never surrender to a lover the ardent soul that she keeps for her paintings.

These four alone, boldly conceived and subtly drawn, would, with their amours and their intrigues, be enough to fill one large, rich novel. Around them move other men and women, grouped in families, in cults, in secret societies, linked by hatreds and ambitions and secrets, driven together momentarily by passionate whims, separated by cruelly comic accidents. Some of them are:

Darley, a poor and feckless poet, living in Egypt as a hack schoolmaster and trying to write, but failing—partly because he cannot organize his powers and partly because he is bemused by love affairs, and drugs, and loneliness;

Melissa Artemis, a Smyrniot night club dancer, Darley's lover for a time;

Pombal, a French diplomat longing for a better post. Darley shares his apartment and some of his girls;

Lieutenant Commander Joshua Scobie, an aged British eccentric who has drifted into the Egyptian Police. The comic counterpart of Bulldog Drummond, he is the clown who makes everyone laugh because he is so vulgar and ineffective, and yet he provokes something like affection;

Mnemjian, a gossipy barber straight out of *A Thousand and One Nights*. He knows everyone, and shaves both the quick and the dead;

Pursewarden, a passionate and embittered British novelist, as direct and fearless as Dylan Thomas but haunted by a special guilt which drives him to his death;

Capodistria, the sexual champion of Alexandria (and therefore called Da Capo);

and the two most powerful characters in the novels, the brothers *Hosnani*—Nessim and Narouz: wealthy, brave, and oppressed members of one of the oldest Christian societies in the world, the Coptic Church. The central story of the four Alexandrian novels deals with a dangerous intrigue which not only wrecks their lives but molds the history of the entire Middle East.

Lawrence Durrell brings his characters to life more vividly and convincingly than all but a handful of novelists in the past fifty years. His Alexandrians live lives which are confused, ardent, and difficult, but continuously interesting and often painfully and dangerously exciting. Love both licit and illicit, and intrigue both personal and political—these are their chief concerns. Being human, they cannot live without love. Being Alexandrians, they cannot live without intrigue.

At first we see them mainly as lovers. Love, for these men and women, does not usually mean happiness or spiritual fulfillment. Often it is a cruel joke played on them by an unseen force. ("Romantic Love—the Comic Demon!" Pursewarden called it.) Sometimes it is an evil necessity—like a drug to an addict who knows that drug-taking will kill him but believes he cannot survive even a day without his regular dosage. Occasionally love is a bitter duel between enemies who happen to be of different sexes. Often it is a caprice, coming and going too suddenly to deserve remorse or create

DURRELL'S ALEXANDRIA:

CARNIVAL

The maddest aberrations of the city now come boldly forward under the protection of the invisible lords of Misrule who preside at this season. No sooner has darkness fallen than the maskers begin to appear in the streets. . . . Everywhere they spring up in the pale moonlight, cowled like monks. The disguise gives them all a gloomy fanatical uniformity of outline which startles the white-robed Egyptians and fills them with alarm—the thrill of a fear which spices the wild laughter pouring out of the houses, carried by the light offshore winds towards the cafés on the seafront; a gaiety which by its very shrillness seems to tremble always upon the edge of madness. . . .

The jazz pouring up from the cellars displaces the tranquil winter air in the parks and thoroughfares, mingling as it reaches the sealine with the drumming perhaps of a liner's screws in the deepwater reaches of the estuary. Or you may hear and see for a brief moment the rip and slither of fireworks against a sky which for a moment curls up at the edges and blushes, like a sheet of burning carbon paper: wild laughter which mixes with the hoarse mooing of an old ship outside the harbour bar—like a cow locked outside a gate.

"The lover fears the carnival" says the proverb. And with the emergence of these black-robed creatures of the night everywhere, all is subtly altered. The whole temperature of life in the city alters, grows warm with the subtle intimations of spring. *Carni vale*—the flesh's farewell to the year, unwinding its mummy wrappings of sex, identity and name, and stepping forward naked into futurity of the dream. . . .

But what stamps the carnival with its spirit of pure mischief is the velvet domino—conferring upon its wearers the disguise which each man in his secret heart desires above all. To become anonymous in an anonymous crowd, revealing neither sex nor relationship nor even facial expression —for the mask of this demented friar's habit leaves only two eyes, glowing like the eyes of a Moslem woman or a bear. . . . Nothing else to distinguish one by; the thick folds of the blackness conceal even the contours of the body. Everyone becomes hipless, breastless, faceless. And concealed beneath the carnival habit (like a criminal desire in the heart, a temptation impossible to resist, an impulse which seems preordained) lie the germs of something: of a freedom which man has seldom dared to imagine for himself. One feels free in this disguise to do whatever one likes without prohibition. All the best murders in the city, all the most tragic cases of mistaken identity, are the fruit of the yearly carnival; while most love affairs begin or end during these three days and nights during which we are delivered from the thrall of personality, from the bondage of ourselves. Once inside that velvet cape and hood, and wife loses husband, husband wife, lover the beloved.

Balthazar, 1958

COPTIC FESTIVAL

Trumpets and drums sounded and there came a rush of horsemen in conical hats waving wooden swords and shrieking in high voices, like women. The camel-and-horse races were due to start. Good, thought I, I shall have a look at that; but treading unwarily I came upon a grotesque scene which I would gladly have avoided if I had been able. The camels of Narouz were being cut up for the feast. Poor things, they knelt there peacefully with their forelegs folded under them like cats while a horde of men attacked them with axes in the moonlight. My blood ran cold, yet I could not tear myself away from this extraordinary spectacle. The animals made no move to avoid the blows, uttered no cries as they were dismembered. The axes bit into them, as if their great bodies were made of cork, sinking deep under every thrust. Whole members were being hacked off as painlessly, it seemed, as when a tree is pruned. The children were dancing about in the moonlight picking up the fragments and running off with them into the lighted town, great gobbets of bloody meat. The camels stared hard at the moon and said nothing. Off came the legs, out came the entrails; lastly the heads would topple under the axe like statuary and lie there in the sand with open eyes. The men doing the axeing were shouting and bantering as they worked. A huge soft carpet of black blood spread into the dunes around the group and the barefoot boys carried the print of it back with them into the township.

Mountolive, 1959

---

regret. Yet always, whether agonizingly painful or unreasonably wanton, love intensifies life. Chic, intelligent, opulently wealthy and brilliantly talented, the people of Durrell's novels are all unsatisfied, all explorers looking, almost in despair, for a life-purpose. In love, be it ever so irrational or cruel, they find it.

I had fallen *in love* [so wrote Justine's first husband]. The very thought filled me with an inexplicable despair and disgust. It was as if I unconsciously realized that in her I had met my evil genius. . . . I thought once of trying to end this attachment, but in every smile and kiss of Justine I felt my resolutions founder. Yet with her one felt all around the companionship of shadows which invaded life and filled it with a new resonance.

Sometimes love is a disease—one of those all-but-inevitable maladies, like acne for adolescents. The sufferer from such a love must pray to live through it; he can receive no help from his friends, only sympathy and (when he recovers) congratulatory joy. So the shrewd doctor, Balthazar, having fallen in love (*in love!*) with a nobly featured young Greek actor who was both handsome and petty, charming and venal, wrecked his own health and his career in service

to his love and finally attempted suicide. "It was," he said, "as if I wanted to drain the sore of love until it healed."

Sometimes, although rarely, love is the highest assertion of life. It is higher even than art. Although art is meant to outlast the individual, to be public and permanent while love is private and temporary, yet art in Durrell's novels is never wholly satisfying either to him who makes it or to those who try to enjoy it. It never says everything. But love, now and then, for a few hours, outdoes art and challenges death. So, as a German air raid begins over Alexandria, Clea says to Darley, "Let us go to bed together and ignore the loutish reality of the world." And so it was.

Love-making itself became a kind of challenge to the whirlwind outside which beat and pounded like a thunderstorm of guns and sirens, igniting the pale skies of the city with the magnificence of its lightning flashes. And kisses themselves became charged with the deliberate affirmation which can come only from the foreknowledge and presence of death. It would have been good to die at any moment then, for love and death had somewhere joined hands.

Durrell's tetralogy of novels, then, presents the Alexandrians first as lovers. They appear first in *Justine*. The time, it would seem, is 1934 or 1935. They are all engaged in an elaborate love ballet. Justine herself, beautiful and elegant, is the wife of the rich Copt, Nessim Hosnani. She is already notorious in the city because of a strange novel written by her first husband, which describes her complex and dangerous character. (Significantly, she is named after the most famous heroine of the Marquis de Sade.) She herself cares nothing for her reputation, but two early injuries afflict her. Once she had a child, a girl, who disappeared, perhaps kidnapped, when only six; now the girl may be a beggar, or a slave in a children's brothel. Long before that, in her youth, Justine herself was raped by a cunning and ruthless sensualist. Perhaps because of that Justine can never truly love anyone; although she passes through the arms of Darley and of other men, or Clea and perhaps of other women, she neither possesses them nor is possessed. "Nymphomania," wrote a friend of her first husband, "may be considered another form of virginity . . . and as for Justine, she may have never have been in love." So the ballet continues: Justine with Darley; Darley with Melissa; Melissa with her discarded lover, old Cohen; Melissa lonely with Nessim in despair . . . until suddenly, unexpectedly, unreasonably, Capodistria, the man who raped Justine, is killed in a silly hunting accident. At once Justine leaves her husband and her lovers to join a *kibbutz* in Palestine; the episode is over.

Yet no episode is over, as long as there are those who remember it. Years later, on a lonely Greek island, the poet Darley recalled Justine and her cruelties and caprices and sufferings. He re-examined the Alexandrians whom he had known. He wrote down all that he could recapture and sent it to his friend Balthazar. It was the novel *Justine*.

To his astonishment, Balthazar brought it back, elaborately annotated and amplified. Only a little of the story had been told in Darley's first attempt. Now much more emerges, in particular, the character of Nessim Hosnani and his intimates: his mother, Leila (once beautiful, now marred forever by smallpox), his strong ugly brother, Narouz, and the other great families of Coptic Christendom. They form a small group called the Cabal, devoted to the study of occult philosophy. Also involved in the group is Pursewarden, and it slowly becomes clear that he is employed by the British intelligence service. These are the people who emerge most clearly in the second novel, *Balthazar*. It ends with a rousing description of the carnival and with a deliciously gruesome murder, but it leaves many problems unsolved.

They are unraveled in the third novel, *Mountolive*. Here, in a story more directly told, we penetrate below the polished film of society and through the perfumed silk of sexual intrigue into the graver world of international politics. David Mountolive knew the Hosnanis first when he was a young diplomat learning Arabic (he had a brief passionate affair with their mother, Leila). Now he returns to Egypt as the British Ambassador and finds the Hosnanis involved in a complicated and dangerous plot. The British government, with characteristic shortsightedness, is bent on building up "Arab unity." The Moslems in Egypt, filled with new strength and aggressive energy, have been systematically suppressing and humiliating the Copts—although (or, perhaps, because) the Copts are the true ancient Egyptians, members of a venerable Christian church, a group so long-established that they regard the Moslems as either intruders or renegades. Therefore, as a counterforce to the Arabs, the Copts are now (1936 or so) supporting the Jewish underground in Palestine. They regard the state of Israel, though still unborn, as the only power which can deliver them and other oppressed minorities from the arrogant exclusiveness of the growing Arab alliance. They supply the Jewish Committee with money and, far more important, with weapons. Nessim, who has contacts on high levels throughout Europe, buys munitions from Sweden and—dramatic irony—from Nazi Germany, and smuggles them into Palestine.

The plot is, perhaps inevitably, discovered by British military intelligence and revealed, however reluctantly, to the Egyptian government by Mountolive in his official role. Some of the results: Pursewarden kills himself because he was Nessim's friend and had tried to conceal the operation which it was his duty to report; we discover that Nessim married Justine *because* she is Jewish, so that the Jewish underground leaders will trust him although he is Christian. And then comes a piece of delicate Oriental intrigue. The plot discovered, Nessim Hosnani must safeguard himself. The Egyptian Minister of the Interior (half pale Albanian, half smoky Nubian) can be bought—the gift is a rare copy of the sacred Koran interleaved with Swiss bank drafts. But to accept a bribe and then do nothing whatever—that is too obvious for a wily pasha. Nessim is permitted to go free; but his brother,

---

DURRELL'S ALEXANDRIA:

THE COUNTRYSIDE

Ancient lands, in all their prehistoric intactness: lake-solitudes hardly brushed by the hurrying feet of the centuries, where the uninterrupted pedigrees of pelican and ibis and heron evolve their slow destinies in complete seclusion. Clover patches of green baize swarming with snakes and clouds of mosquitoes. A landscape devoid of songbirds yet full of owls, hoopoes and kingfishers hunting by day, pluming themselves on the banks of the tawny waterways. The packs of half-wild dogs foraging, the blindfolded water-buffaloes circling the water-wheels in an eternity of darkness. The little wayside chancels built of dry mud and floored with fresh straw where the pious traveller might say a prayer as he journeyed. Egypt! The goose-winged sails scurrying along the freshets with perhaps a human voice singing a trailing snatch of song. The click-click of the wind in the Indian corn, plucking at the coarse leaves, scumbling them. Liquid mud exploded by rainstorms in the dust-laden air throwing up mirages everywhere, despoiling perspectives. A lump of mud swells to the size of a man, a man to the size of a church. Whole segments of the sky and land displace, open like a lid, or heel over on their side to turn upside down. Flocks of sheep walk in and out of these twisted mirrors, appearing and disappearing, goaded by the quivering nasal cries of invisible shepherds. A great confluence of pastoral images from the forgotten history of the old world which still lives on side by side with the one we have inherited.

Clea, 1960

---

the other Hosnani, who lives far out on the desert edge, is executed by anonymous and untraceable murderers. *Mountolive* ends with a superb description of the funeral of Narouz, celebrated with rituals even more ancient than those of the ancient Coptic Church.

All this happened in the late 1930's.

Darley looks back upon it in *Justine, Balthazar,* and *Mountolive*. In the fourth and final novel of the group, *Clea*, he returns to the close, vibrant world of Alexandria during World War II to find that much he had believed about his friends was false—or, if it was true, had been falsified by time and the pressure of events. There is no stable truth.

Pursewarden, the brilliant writer, is a case in point. In the earlier novels we see him as flippant, gay, heartless. He loves many women and is faithful to none. We know that he is separated from his wife, and in one idyllic scene we see him waltzing in the London snow with his blind sister, Liza, to celebrate, he says, the birthday of the poet William Blake. Pursewarden kills himself. At first, in *Justine*, his suicide is understood to be the result of maudlin self-distrust: he was unsure of his art. Then, in *Balthazar*, it is put down as al-

PASSAGES FROM THE FOUR NOVELS QUOTED BY PERMISSION OF E. P. DUTTON & COMPANY, INC., NEW YORK.

most play-acting: the wish to score a final unbeatable effect. In *Mountolive* it is interpreted more seriously, as the self-elimination of an officer who had failed in his duty. ("Utter folly!" cries Mountolive angrily. "Nobody kills himself for an official reason!") Now at last, in *Clea*, the final motive appears. Although married, Pursewarden had always been in love with his own sister, the blind and beautiful Liza. He even had a daughter by her. When Liza fell in love with Mountolive and seemed to be about to enter a true and honest and complete marriage, Pursewarden—

But why does anyone do anything final or desperate? Is there ever a single reason? Shall we ever know the truth about the actions of anyone, even ourselves?

Lawrence Durrell's tetralogy is a search for the truth, and an exercise in relativity. His chief model in this is Marcel Proust. In Proust we go through a long series of discoveries, sometimes appealing, sometimes comically disgusting. We find that the handsome young nobleman is in fact a pervert, that the cheap call-girl becomes a great lady, that the boring old pedant wins a Nobel Prize, that society itself, apparently a structure as firm and symmetrical as a baroque palace, is riddled with underground passages where monstrous criminals lurk; that it is constantly collapsing and being rebuilt by the most unlikely parvenus or amateurs, and that neither ancient blood nor noble character can guarantee survival and success.

The relationships in Durrell's Alexandria are no less intricate and elusive than those in Proust's Paris. Men and women change. They misunderstand their own emotions, or disguise them. At a given time, they act thus and so. A week later, they deny what they did. A month later, they forget the facts, the motives, and the results. A year later, they have created an entirely new set of truths; the original has been lost, even for those who acted in it. Only art can, sometimes, seize some moments of the truth. And so Lawrence Durrell, with his elegantly perceptive style, has grasped some moments in the lives of some bright, dangerous, and elusive people. His ear for urgent dialogue, his eye for exotic landscapes and excited crowd scenes, are faultless; his prose has a vividness and a clangor which mark him, among novelists, as a true poet.

We are tempted, as we read the Alexandrian novels, to ask how far they are purely imagination and how far they are hints, penetrable disguises, partial revelations of a truth which is meant to be discovered. The poor unsuccessful poet who observes these strange adventures, and sometimes assists in them, is called Darley, a name which is not too unlike Durrell. Even his initials are revealed in a joke by Pursewarden, who mocks old L.G.D. in a phrase from Blake ("Lineaments of Gratified Desire"). And Darley retires to a quiet Greek island with a little girl whom he brings up in love and loneliness. From *Who's Who* and other books of reference we learn that Mr. Durrell's full name is Lawrence George Durrell, that he was for some time press attaché of the British Embassy in Alexandria, and that at some time before 1955 he was living a hermitlike existence on Cyprus with his small daughter.

There are some kinds of fiction—especially those investigative, introspective novels such as Proust's *Remembrance of Things Past*—in which the author himself seems to play a part although he maintains the conventional pretense that he is outside the book. Perhaps one of the central pleasures of Mr. Durrell's Alexandrian tetralogy is that of penetrating through the fiction to the substratum of fact and then admiring the blend of the two. There are some men who have led difficult and distorted lives, and who at length acquire the accumulated experience and the practiced talent to write what they have seen and felt and thought. What they write can hardly be called fiction, for it is not pure invention; nor can it be called fact, for it is shaped and decorated. However extravagant, however painful, however intricate, both the lives of these men and their books are truly works of art.

CIRCLE IN THE SQUARE

CONTINUED FROM PAGE 99

has spread that down in the Village and east of the Village are several clusters of small theaters engaged in putting on plays which their proprietors admire, the almost forgotten pastime of theater shopping has risen again in New York.

Because of the physical limitations of its former house, the Circle in the Square has also been a leader in liberating the contemporary stage from conventional and often competitively ostentatious notions of what constitutes a professional theatrical production. A well-equipped modern theater is a machine of almost limitless versatility, but complete freedom of means is not synonymous with the highest vitality. It is not just that the theater can produce an excellent illusion of reality (though a preoccupation with literal accuracy in sets and stage deportment often diminishes our drama); it is also that it can master almost any illusion. When audiences applaud a set as the curtain rises, they betray themselves. How can they possibly know that it is a good set until they have seen the play for which it was built? Have they come to some modern equivalent of the Destruction of Pompeii? Illusion is essentially the prerogative of the playwright and his company, and the theater becomes mere playfulness when the designers take over the magic.

Off-Broadway is financially poor and physically makeshift; illusion is not easily achieved, but when it comes, it is from the right source. No one applauds when the curtain rises at the Circle in the Square. For one thing, there is no curtain; for another, there is nothing on view to excite the most volatile hand slapper. Placed about on stage there may be a few chairs and tables, perhaps a rug to designate a living area, a hanging lamp to light a dining table, leaf-twined trellis sections tacked up to mark a garden, a stepladder if action is to proceed on a second floor. All this is mere lumber, lifeless until the actors bring in the illusion. Then, however, the possibilities are limited only by the play's power to initiate illusion and the spectators' power to respond.

The necessity for both actors and audience to share commitment in the terms of the play is what so often gives the off-Broadway play an almost hypnotic vitality. Attendance at the Circle in the Square is not a spectator sport; what your ticket buys is the right to take part in an exercise of the imagination. But this does not mean that the Circle's facilities are a triumph of theater architecture. As in many of the off-Broadway houses, the stage of both the old and new Circle in the Square theaters is an adaptation to available circumstances of theater-in-the-round. In the first Circle theater the audience sat around three sides of the dance floor of the one-time night club, in slightly elevated tiers. The performers and spectators, virtually unseparated, were quite close to one another. The fourth side of the floor was blank, actually a series of shuttered loft doors, which gave on the street. This provided the players with a wall which, figuratively and sometimes literally, they could back up to (often it was dressed with skeletal scenery). The Circle's directors became so happy with this arrangement that they have almost exactly duplicated it in their new home.

This design is greatly superior to true theater-in-the-round, which, whatever its advantages of salable seat space, deprives a production of any tangible orientation and usually involves the actors in a melancholy vortical movement that resembles the slow emptying of a sink. The Circle's wall is a boon; the actor has thus a podium and a refuge; he can gaze "out there" without staring some cash customer out of countenance. Still, for the audience, this design does away with "upstage" or "downstage," with "stage left" or "stage right"—it all depends on where you are sitting.

Relative position is a powerful tool in the theater, and a director deprived of it must develop a new style of his own. One reason for the Circle's long survival is the style that José Quintero devised to suit his hand-me-down theater arrangement. And, to flip the coin, the Circle's former primitive stage in a night club became the springboard from which Quintero has leaped in a very few years into the small circle of "name" directors. These are the men—Harold Clurman, Robert Lewis, Elia Kazan, are prominent among them— whose services are bid for by Broadway producers and who, by selecting the plays they choose to undertake, affect the quality and direction of the commercial theater. Gaining critical acclaim for his work at the Circle, Quintero has been sought out as director for such varied prestige productions as *I Pagliacci* and *Cavalleria Rusticana* at the Metropolitan Opera, Jane Bowles's play *In the Summer House* for Broadway, and Robinson Jeffers's *Medea* on television.

The influences that Quintero acknowledges as having exerted the most influence upon him are the Catholic Church and Martha Graham. In this context, he refers to the pageantry of the Church, and once you know the source, the logic of the adaptation can be startling. Despite the surface incongruity of the notion, the spatial arrangements at the old Circle, re-created at the new, are not unlike those of a cathedral. Quintero does not assemble his performance on a box platform to confront a massed audience. He has one axis of action to work with and it passes through the center of his spectators. One does not think in terms of entrances left or right. Players emerge from the darkness onto the stage from various entrances, including those the audience enters by. The analogies with church procedure here are obvious enough. Situated thus in the midst of his audience, Quintero can use processions, opposed choirs, leader and chorus, wedges aimed to threaten or defend a focal point. These assemblages convey universally understood implications, and they say the same thing from whatever the point of observation. The effect sounds stiff when the forms are thus isolated, but Quintero rarely employs his geometry bare; like the sculptor's armature, it is the framework about which he constructs his play, articulating its parts into a communicative and subtly moving whole.

He also has a way of flinging his performers into the playing area like pebbles flung from a hand, a brilliantly effective way of swinging a scene instantly into full momentum or, alternately, of pitching the action to a blink of frozen suspense before climax. This device owes more, perhaps, to Greek than to Gothic sources, or it may be a link with Martha Graham. The most obvious contribution of the great dancer is the high plasticity, or consciousness of himself as sculpture, that Quintero requires of an actor. Actors who are given no front or back for their impersonations are forced to be peculiarly aware of themselves in three dimensions. The twist of a back, the jut of an elbow, or the slope of a shoulder must all be simultaneously considered, for each of them is going to convey the dominant impression to some segment of the audience. In a sense a Circle performance is theater-as-sculpture rather than theater-as-mural.

The modified theater-in-the-round productions at the Circle result in performances that seem uncommonly fluid. Either in spite of or because of an almost embarrassing intimacy between audience and actors, the latter radiate a heightened aliveness that lends them stature. It is a lyric, impressionistic theater, very sensitive to emotional pressure, very responsive to shifting winds. It is necessarily—and by Quintero's choice—a poetic, allusive theater: it cannot be realistic, though it often deals in realism.

The limitations that had done much to form this admirable style were nonetheless limitations: no loft from which to fly scenery, no bridge behind a proscenium from which to direct lights; in short, almost no apparatus for illusion save talent. Over the years, Quintero had to learn what he must forego, but the Circle still made mistakes. If *The Iceman Cometh,* that rambling juggernaut of impotent glory, could be triumphantly staged there (May, 1956–February, 1958), why should Brendan Behan's *The Quare Fellow* (November, 1958–March, 1959), also rambling, also self-consuming and impotent, fail to succeed? The answer in part is that the brilliant counterpoint of speech in *The Iceman* was perfectly suited to staging in the round. The dialogue skipped and stuttered, swelled and waned; it signaled from table to table in Harry Hope's bar like a flickering swamp fire. Also, the tension of the play builds up steadily to the Homeric jest of Hickey, and the theater's open form was fine for the gyrations of Hickey's *danse macabre.* (The first-row audiences behind little tables were contiguous with the character-patrons of Harry Hope's bar, the show's setting.) Finally, of course, in this case Hickey was Jason Robards, Jr.

The Quare Fellow, by contrast, has a more steady, aching pressure of suspense. It gets its effect by piling one vignette on another to a toppling ironic climax of anticlimax. Scene by scene, it had fine moments at the Circle, but it never took

shape. As a matter of fact, the script was defective in its own structure and would have profited from the formal shape and order that the modern box stage imposes.

Another, quite different, example was Fergusson's experiment adapted from *Huckleberry Finn. The King and the Duke,* a dramatic square dance with charades, was a warm and ingratiating theater diversion. But it did not succeed—partly because the audience found itself for once almost embarrassingly implicated in the proceedings, partly because the music and dances seemed to ask for more spacious and formal accommodations.

When Quintero was asked about the stage on which he had worked for ten years, he smiled a little grimly and remarked that off-Broadway had certainly proved the adage that all the drama needs is two boards and a passion. Two boards are about what most of them can afford. But when he was asked whether he would prefer a conventional, proscenium theater, he said No. What Quintero is trying to approach in his new working place on Bleecker Street is something like the Stratford, Ontario, Shakespearean auditorium, though obviously on a much smaller scale. The Ontario theater is a platform stage almost surrounded by the audience area, but elevated and with a back or inner stage for "closet" scenes.* This arrangement is like having your cake and eating it.

Now as to money, Messrs. Quintero, Mann, and Connell consider themselves professionals and a basic professional obligation is to stay in business. At the beginning, the Circle played virtuoso gymnastics on a shoestring and stayed open, quite simply, by a generous camaraderie that is always heartwarming and always certain to collapse if a spark of success does not catch somewhere. For the Circle, the spark was *Summer and Smoke,* which brought fame to Geraldine Page and for the first time a perceptible reserve in the bank account. Two plays later (Victor Wolfson's *American Gothic* failed; Capote's *The Grass Harp* was financially a stand-off, though it earned a good deal of prestige, which it had failed to do on Broadway), Fire Commissioner Cavanaugh padlocked the premises at the start of what looked like an almost indefinite run for *The Girl on the Via Flaminia.* Reluctantly the management ventured to move *Via Flaminia* uptown, but it failed to take hold in the harsh commercial soil of Broadway. For a time this threatened to end the Circle in the Square. Quintero was engaged to direct a Broadway production of *Portrait of a Lady;* Mann took a job as assistant stage manager with *The Bad Seed;* Connell set off exploring new theatrical areas. But none was happy, and soon they decided to try independent production once more. Mann came back to New York to find a theater (and some rehearsal money). But the old Greenwich Village Inn was still empty and still the only possibility in sight; this time they were able to convince the Fire Department that they could operate it within the safety laws. The institution

*See illustrations to "The Theater Breaks Out of Belasco's Box" by Walter Kerr in HORIZON for July. 1959.

was running again, after only a broken stride. Quintero was again its director; old colleague Connell hurried to rejoin it.

In its second materialization, the Circle has operated with more conventional bookkeeping, but still within limits that would not please an accountant. Accountants admire a little reserve fat, and off-Broadway is a lean world. Here are the basic figures for a typical production at the new Circle in the Square. It costs $8,000 to $10,000 to mount the play—rehearsals, costumes, promotion, plant overhead, etc. Once running, the weekly break-even figure is around $3,000 and the maximum gross in the 200-seat house is $4,500. That means the theater must run at 67 per cent capacity to stay even and must do, for example, 90 per cent for ten weeks to accumulate the kitty for the next production.

Such figures suggest this is no business for tycoons, and in fact the Circle management has survived in recent years by extramural work. After the revival of *The Iceman* had won grateful cheers from critics and public, O'Neill's widow entrusted *Long Day's Journey into Night* to Quintero's direction and to the management of Quintero, Mann, and Connell for a Broadway presentation. This made what is called real money, and although it contributed nothing directly to the Circle's solvency, it did for a time allow the owners to keep their own fingers from the Circle's till by paying them liberal salaries for their Broadway work. Last summer Quintero staged *Macbeth* with Siobhan McKenna and Jason Robards, Jr., for the Cambridge Drama Festival, and the Circle in the Square triumvirate is hopeful of bringing it to Broadway. All last autumn Mann, Quintero, and Connell engaged in legal skirmishing to bring Bertold Brecht's *Mother Courage* to Broadway with Miss McKenna in the title role. Broadway, in short, is where the Circle looks to cultivate its cash crop.

But why accept the limitations of the present setup; why indeed work off Broadway at all? A bigger theater (moderately bigger; the Phoenix is immense and so are its headaches) would seem to be the answer. A house of about 500 seats, says Mann, would be ideal (the smallest Broadway theater holds about 750). But in Mann's ideal house, the overhead could very easily mount as fast as the gross. Union demands would be stiffer, both in base scale and in the number of technical jobs made obligatory; rent and associated expenses would leap. At this level financing would become a much more formidable problem, and off-Broadway might begin to depend on the same kind of speculative money that has dominated the theater uptown in recent years.

Obviously the directors of the Circle in the Square are not refugees from Broadway; on the contrary, Broadway found them in Sheridan Square. But they have only made safaris uptown and they prefer to maintain their explorer role. Up on Broadway they are hired hands, or at best operators of one-shot enterprises. Giddy and exciting as the experience can be, and lucrative when all goes well, it is for them not as satisfying as running their own theater in their own way.

The Circle in the Square has moved, but it is still in Greenwich Village, with its traditions and its hungry audiences.

Actually, the permanence of the house (if not a repertory company, then at least a repertory management) is what principally distinguishes an off-Broadway theater like the Circle in the Square from the uptown business. There is no essential difference in the plays produced; often they are the same plays, but offered in revival for their dramatic rather than their box office, star-vehicle values. The Circle management is not avant-garde; it is, if anything, conservative and has been criticized for a lack of experimental daring. But Mann points out that the arcane play, the antidrama or abstract morality that "couldn't possibly attract an audience uptown," has proved equally incapable of attracting an audience downtown. However that may be, the taste of this management is for solid accomplishment rather than for novelty; the three men would rather put on revivals of neglected classics or restage good plays that stumbled on Broadway than man the artistic barricades.

This may be a shortcoming, but they have not done badly as artists over the past ten years. They brought O'Neill back to his big public; they have offered Anouilh, Lorca, Giraudoux, Benavente, Williams, Capote; they did real service (and made money) by resurrecting Edwin Justus Mayer's forgotten *Children of Darkness;* they backed their convictions to produce *The Quare Fellow* when Broadway wanted no traffic with Behan.

Many of the Circle's friends wish they could find new playwrights, and so do they themselves; in fact they are vehement about it, for they know that they cannot forever feed their theater from the files. In this respect, they are somewhat trapped; their standards are not unlike the best Broadway standards, and Broadway uses a fairly fine sieve. An old playwright who promises to write new plays for them is Thornton Wilder. Impressed with their record even before their revival of *Our Town,* Wilder is writing for the Circle a cycle of one-acters to be called *The Seven Deadly Sins.* But a living theater cannot be content with the contribution of acceptable, older masters; it demands fresh talent on which to nurture itself.

Perhaps a willingness to experiment, even sacrifice, is the price the Circle will have to pay for new voices, and perhaps the economics of their new theater will permit an occasional bet on promise. The contemporary success and usefulness of the Circle in the Square are now more matters of fact than opinion. But the theater's ultimate reputation, its place in the annals, will depend primarily on the writers it brings to public notice. In a sense, Mann, Quintero, and Connell are anticipatory members of a partnership; the other is that O'Casey, that O'Neill of our day who has yet to appear.

A regular playgoer both on and off Broadway, Robert Hatch is literary editor of The Nation. *He relieves Harold Clurman as its drama critic, but more frequently reviews films.*

Lead, Kindly Light, Amid the Encircling Semantic Fog
OR
Through the Unrotated Centroid with Gun and Jealousy Factor

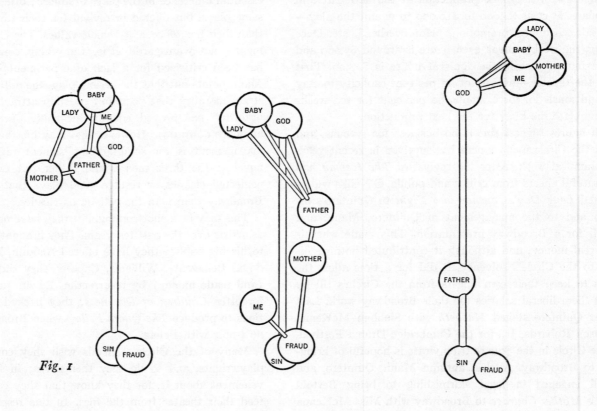

Fig. 1

Every world has its underprivileged, and among the scientists it is becoming increasingly evident that the unhappy ones are those who deal with man and the way he talks, or to use their own nomenclature, the anthropologists and semanticists. To speak candidly, they are mad with envy. What turns them a bright, pulsating green is the beautiful exactness of other sciences. They look upon the mathematicians with their orderly little numbers and tidy theorems, the engineers with their exquisite drawings, the chemists with their formulas and snappy retorts, and the endocrinologists with their—well, endocrinology, and imitate them as best they can. It is an uphill battle against a shifty and downright unreliable subject: people, every last one of them as variable as the wind, are apt to lapse into wrongthink or old-speak or some other foolishness just when you think you have them classified. But semanticists never give up, of course, and we have a report here on activities at the front, with something for every endomorph, mesomorph, and ectomorph in the family.

Our first body blow to the older scientists comes from a book called *The Measurement of Meaning* by Charles E. Osgood and two associates at the University of Illinois. Pacing ahead of the field in the jargon sweepstakes, they have worked up a statistical process called the Quartimax Rotation of the Centroid (*sings, doesn't it?*) which tests words from *Roget's Thesaurus* (for instance, sacred-profane, wet-dry, rumbling-whining) in an ILLIAC computer and finds that the three most significant dimensions of semantic space are Evaluation, Potency, and Activity, unless it is the other way around. Laying the Quartimax aside, the authors deduce arguments as sweet as any theorem in geometry:

Whenever some stimulus other than the significate is contiguous with the significate, it will acquire an increment of association with some portion of the total behavior elicited by the significate as a representational mediation process.

Match that, Euclid.

But these big, cold principles have their warm, personal applications, or individual conceptual structures, even as you and I. An example appears in Fig. 1 (above), showing how a given person, in this case a female psychiatric patient, places a given idea in relation to other ideas. Here are the patterns, according to Osgood, made by such concepts as "me," "baby," and "God" in her mind before, during, and after therapy. "Me" and "Mother" moved pretty close to the sin and fraud goalposts at the height of the doctor's ministrations, but in the end it was "Father" who scored. Well, that's how the quartimax rotates.

Osgood says in concluding the book, "It would be foolish to begin collecting data for a functional dictionary of connotative meanings when the factor structure remains unclear and obviously insufficient, and the nature of the concept-scale interaction is still obscure," but over here among the anthropologists they are stealing a march on him. Edward T. Hall, an anthropologist and former State Department Point Four operative, has got the whole business pinned down. In his book *The Silent Language*, he concludes that what musical scores did for music, someone must do for all the behavior patterns that make up our culture. In fact, the undaunted anthropologist has prepared a vade mecum for us all, called "A Map of Culture." *Voilà* your concept-scale

A MAP OF CULTURE

Primary Message Systems	Interactional 0	Organizational 1	Economic 2	Sexual 3	Territorial 4	Temporal 5	Instructional 6	Recreational 7	Protective 8	Exploitational 9
Interaction 0	Communication Vocal qualifiers Kinesics Language 00	Status and Role 01	Exchange 02	How the sexes interact 03	Places of interaction 04	Times of interaction 05	Teaching and learning 06	Participation in the arts and sports (active and passive) 07	Protecting and being protected 08	Use of telephones, signals, writing, etc. 09
Association 1	Community 10	Society Class Caste Government 11	Economic roles 12	Sexual roles 13	Local group roles 14	Age group roles 15	Teachers and learners 16	Entertainers and athletes 17	Protectors (doctors, clergy, soldiers, police, etc.) 18	Use of group property 19
Subsistence 2	Ecological community 20	Occupational groupings 21	Work Formal work Maintenance Occupations 22	Sexual division of labor 23	Where the individual eats, cooks, etc. 24	When the individual eats, cooks, etc. 25	Learning from working 26	Pleasure from working 27	Care of health, protection of livelihood 28	Use of foods, resources, and equipment 29
Bisexuality 3	Sex community (clans, sibs) 30	Marriage groupings 31	Family 32	The Sexes Masc. vs. Fem. Sex (biological) Sex (technical) 33	Areas assigned to individuals by virtue of sex 34	Periods assigned to individuals by virtue of sex 35	Teaching and learning sex roles 36	Participation in recreation by sex 37	Protection of sex and fertility 38	Use of sex differentiating decoration and adornment 39
Territoriality 4	Community territory 40	Group territory 41	Economic areas 42	Men's and women's territories 43	Space Formal space Informal space Boundaries 44	Scheduling of space 45	Teaching and learning individual space assignments 46	Fun, playing games, etc., in terms of space 47	Privacy 48	Use of fences and markers 49
Temporality 5	Community cycles 50	Group cycles 51	Economic cycles 52	Men's and women's cyclical activities 53	Territorially determined cycles 54	Time Sequence Cycles Calendar 55	When the individual learns 56	When the individual plays 57	Rest, vacations, holidays 58	Use of time-telling devices, etc. 59
Learning 6	Community lore—what gets taught and learned 60	Learning groups—educational institutions 61	Reward for teaching and learning 62	What the sexes are taught 63	Places for learning 64	Scheduling of learning (group) 65	Enculturation Rearing Informal learning Education 66	Making learning fun 67	Learning self-defense and to stay healthy 68	Use of training aids 69
Play 7	Community play—the arts and sports 70	Play groups—teams and troupes 71	Professional sports and entertainment 72	Men's and women's play, fun, and games 73	Recreational areas 74	Play seasons 75	Instructional play 76	Recreation Fun Playing Games 77	Exercise 78	Use of recreational materials (playthings) 79
Defense 8	Community defenses—structured defense systems 80	Defense groups—armies, police, public health, organized religion 81	Economic patterns of defense 82	What the sexes defend (home, honor, etc.) 83	What places are defended 84	The When of defense 85	Scientific, religious, and military training 86	Mass exercises and military games 87	Protection Formal defenses Informal defenses Technical defenses 88	Use of materials for protection 89
Exploitation 9	Communication networks 90	Organizational networks (cities, building groups, etc.) 91	Food, resources, and industrial equipment 92	What men and women are concerned with and own 93	Property—what is enclosed, counted, and measured 94	What periods are measured and recorded 95	School buildings, training aids, etc. 96	Amusement and sporting goods and their industries 97	Fortifications, armaments, medical equipment, safety devices 98	Material Systems Contact w/ environment Motor habits Technology 99

Fig. 2

FROM *The Silent Language* © 1959 EDWARD T. HALL, PUBLISHED BY DOUBLEDAY

interactions, Osgood! It's all there in Hall's Fig. 2, and it will relate anything. Hall and his colleague George L. Trager operated, they say, "on the assumption that culture was bio-basic and had its well-springs in a number of infra-cultural activities." No sooner had this apple fallen on their heads, so to speak, than they started constructing their map, or grid. On one side are what the authors call Primary Message Systems, familiar old messages like Exploitation, Territoriality, and, as Kinsey taught us, Bisexuality, messages that reach every red-blooded American. At the top are their sturdy adjectival counterparts. What sort of message do we get from "Bisexuality—Organizational"? We get "Marriage Groupings," naturally. As Mr. Hall tells us, what he has achieved is "a sort of cultural equivalent of the periodic tables of chemistry," and the chemists can put *that* in their pipes and smoke it.

The beauty of all this, as the book says itself, is that "no major categories have been overlooked" in this chart of culture. We did notice that "Poetry," "Literature," and "Writing" were missing from the chart and even from the index of the book. Maybe they are hiding behind "Communication." But we did find "Jokes," and discovered that the matter is pretty well categorized:

Many jokes [Hall says] are based on incongruities of one sort or another, which is one reason why the reader (or listener) has to be almost a native speaker in order to appreciate the full implications of a joke. If he is unable to assess the degree of incongruity, he can't appreciate the humor. The old joke about the girl from Brooklyn trying to put on airs in Schrafft's by ordering "ersters on the half shell" (using a very Bostonian a!) is funny because it is incongruous on several levels. Not only does she use two dialects but switches from substandard usage to what she thinks is upper-class.

There you have it; no mystery to humor after all. It's all there in the formula, rotating on the centroid.

—Oliver Jensen

PHILO-SEMITISM

CONTINUED FROM PAGE 103

given a passport to England. His book was translated, published, and republished there. Then, in 1653, the great moment seemed to have come. In that year the English Rump Parliament, which had made the Dutch war, was turned out by Oliver Cromwell and the "parliament of saints" set up. It was dominated by the "Fifth Monarchy men," the men who (like Vieira) believed that the four world-monarchies of history were about to be succeeded by the messianic monarchy of Christ—and that they had been chosen to usher it in. The parliament of saints marked the high tide of puritan millenarism in England. Cromwell himself was carried away by the infection of prophetic zeal: his speeches became as rhapsodical and fantastic as those of Menasseh himself. In such circumstances Menasseh applied again for the readmission of the Jews, and a new committee was set up to consider his application. Pamphleteers, preachers, even the three "Generals of the Fleet" supported it. And then, suddenly, all hopes were dashed. Cromwell discovered what the English millenarists were up to. He realized that the doctrine of the millennium, at least as advanced by the English "saints," the Fifth Monarchy men, was not merely a mystical aspiration: it cloaked a plan of social revolution, a revolution which he would never countenance. To Cromwell this was a terrible disillusionment. The parliament of saints was dissolved. From that moment the millennium was not to be heard again in English politics. The warm, diffuse fog of mysticism was suddenly condensed. And along with the millennium, it seemed, the hopes of Menasseh and the Jews must also dissolve.

Of all this Menasseh was unaware. Ironically, while the enthusiasm of the English puritans, which had been so warm, was suddenly cooled, that of the Jews, which had been so cool, now began to warm up. By 1655 Oliver Cromwell had become a different man. He no longer believed that a golden age was dawning or that ancient prophecies would be fulfilled in his time. Mistrustful of all idealism, he now concentrated on the dull daily round of practical possibilities. But Menasseh was more visionary than ever. In that year he published an apocalyptic work on Nebuchadnezzar's dream—the same dream which had been the inspiration of Vieira and the English Fifth Monarchists. It was written in Spanish—a sign that it was addressed to gentiles—and was illustrated by a gentile artist, the great painter of Amsterdam Jews and rabbis, including Menasseh himself, Rembrandt. At the same time Menasseh assured his Christian friends that he was more convinced than ever that the Messiah was on his way. From every quarter, he wrote, Christians were supporting him: French Huguenots, German Protestants, Bohemian refugees, "and from England, how many voices!" In the autumn of this same year, Menasseh at last set out for England, armed with a printed appeal for the readmis-

sion of the Jews: an appeal based largely on the grounds that, according to their common Scriptures, the Fifth World Monarchy was now dawning, the Messiah due, the millennium at hand. Thus armed, he arrived in London and presented himself in person before the Lord Protector.

Could any appeal have been worse timed? Fifth Monarchy—the very words were now, to Cromwell, like a red rag to a bull. When he heard them, he could hardly control his speech. To him the words meant communism, anarchy, "blood and confusion," war on society and property; "in so much as if one man had twelve cows, they held another that wanted cows ought to take shares with his neighbour. Who could have said anything was his own if that had gone on?" And yet here was Menasseh seeking the readmission of the Jews on the explicit grounds that they too were Fifth Monarchists! His appeal seemed doomed to failure.

And yet how can any man clear from his mind the deposit of its greatest experience? Cromwell, like Milton, like all his generation, might now be a disillusioned man, but even in their disillusion men cannot escape from their own past and the deep-rooted ideas and sympathies it has engendered. And so, even in their new mood, Cromwell and his friends, the puritan gentry of England, continued to pursue, more cautiously, on a narrower basis, their old aims: and those aims included the reception—no longer a mystical fusion, but a quiet, rational reception—of the Jews.

MILLENNIUM IN THE

The wave of millenarist enthusiasm which (as Mr. Trevor-Roper points out in his article) subsided in Europe around 1660, rolled across the Atlantic to New England. Here it found an eloquent spokesman in Samuel Sewall, the Boston judge who presided over the Salem witchcraft trials and later most honorably repented in Old South Church. In a tract of 1697 entitled *Phaenomena Quaedam Apocalyptica ad Aspectum Novi Orbis Configurata*, Judge Sewall addressed himself to the Biblical injunction that, before the millennium could come, the Lost Sheep must be recovered. To the Jews, of course, this passage applied to the Ten Lost Tribes of Israel, but to Gentiles it meant the conversion of the Jews to Christianity.

It was the belief of Judge Sewall (and other New England Puritans) that the Indians were the missing Ten Tribes and that America was the logical site of the New Jerusalem. But first, he reasoned, the Jews would have to come to the New World and be converted along with the Indians.

In his tract Sewall discusses the presence of Jews in Spanish and Portuguese colonies (where they were disguised as Gentiles) and the West Indian islands, as well as New York and New England. This indicated that they had come to the New World to join with Christians in the One Fold under the One Shepherd of the verse from St. John, Chapter 10: 16,

And other sheep I have, which are not of this fold: them

At the famous Whitehall Conference in December 1655, Cromwell listened to the case for and against the return of the Jews. Since the high tide of mysticism had receded, the solid rocks of Jewish inconvertibility were now painfully clear, but Cromwell's majestic tolerance rose above these difficulties. How could the Jews ever be converted, he asked, if they were kept permanently out of earshot? Finally, when Menasseh's indiscreet language and large claims had reinforced popular prejudice and City jealousy against him, Cromwell withdrew the whole affair from the limelight. He would settle the matter, he said, by himself; and next year he did so. By a quiet, inconspicuous legal ruling that the Spanish crypto-Jews in London were not Spaniards but Jews, and therefore immune from the consequences of his Spanish war, he not only saved their property but, by implication, legitimized their presence. From that moment, not from Menasseh's visit, the Jews were legally readmitted to England. The philo-Semites, in their retreat from messianism, had closed the front door; but the residue of their inspiration was still strong enough to open the back door and leave it permanently ajar. Admittedly, the beneficiaries as yet were few: they were not, after all, the penniless refugees from Poland; they were a few rich Jews from Spain and Portugal, the "King's Jews" of Charles II.

Thus Christian and Jewish messianism, in the end, failed to merge. When one had at last warmed up, the other was becoming cold. By 1660 mystical Protestant philo-Semitism was dead, dead with the generation out of whose now remote experience it had been born. But Jewish messianism still had a few years to run. Menasseh ben Israel died, a year before Cromwell, heartbroken by the failure of his theatrical gestures, but the movement which he represented went on. After all, the great year 1666 was still to come. Between 1649 and 1653 Christian and Jewish messianists alike had looked forward to that year. In 1666, said the English Fifth Monarchist John Rogers, the Saints, having already captured Rome, would conquer the whole world. In that year, said the Portuguese Jesuit Vieira, King John of Portugal would rise from the dead and found, in Lisbon, the Fifth World Monarchy. In that year, said the Jewish cabalists, their Messiah would set up their new monarchy in the Holy Land. When that year came, however, the Fifth Monarchists were scattered and disillusioned, and Vieira was in the hands of the Inquisition, threatened with the stake for his partiality to the Jews. Only the Jews were left with their illusions. When the messianic year came, they had to go it alone.

How they went it alone is another story. It is the story of Sabbatai Zevi, the Levantine Jew who, in 1648, the year of redemption, decided to be the Messiah. In 1666, the messianic year, after long and extravagant preparation in Cairo, Jerusalem, and the ghettos of Europe, he inaugurated his reign with blowing of horns and scenes of wild license in his native city of Smyrna. For a moment of time, all the scattered Jews of Europe were electrified by Sabbatai's high-pressure antics. Grave Sephardic merchants, with the scroll of the Law in their arms, skipped and danced in the Exchanges of Hamburg and Amsterdam; Queen Christina's Jewish banker and her Jewish physician joined the giddy merry-go-round; the old-established Jews of Hungary dismantled their houses and prepared to march to the Holy Land. And the newly settled Jews of London declared that the leaders of the Twelve Tribes of Israel had been sighted off the north of Scotland, bearing toward them in a ship with silken sails and ropes and manned by sailors who spoke the Hebrew tongue. Meanwhile Sabbatai, in Smyrna, was distributing kingdoms and crowns, abrogating the old Law and declaring the new reign of the Messiah.

Before the year was out, the Sultan of Turkey put a summary end to these follies: to escape a more painful alternative, Sabbatai and his wife announced their conversion to Mohammedanism, and their enthusiastic followers were left to explain the *Zohar* and the *Kabbala* away. From that time onward, the basis of Jewish, as of Christian, messianism had crumbled. With it crumbled also the last element in that brief and strange episode, the unique experience of one generation, mystical Christian philo-Semitism.

NEW WORLD: 1697

also I must bring, and they shall hear my voice; and there shall be one fold, and one shepherd

and of the verses from Ezekiel, Chapter 37: 24, 26,

And David my servant shall be king over them; and they all shall have one shepherd: they shall also walk in my judgments, and observe my statutes, and do them. . . . Moreover I will make a covenant of peace with them; it shall be an everlasting covenant with them: and I will place them, and multiply them, and will set my sanctuary in the midst of them for evermore.

In interpreting these verses, Sewall wrote:

Manassah-Ben Israel, Downam, Thorogood, Eliot, and others were of Opinion that America *was first peopled by the Ten Tribes. God's removing* Israel *out of his sight, is no less than three times mentioned; which may insinuate the Remoteness of that Land, into which God by his Providence intended to cast them. And none was so remote, and so much out of sight, as* America. *Mr. Greenhil thinks it is no Hæresie to say, Christ meant the Ten Tribes* John, *10.16. alluding to Ezek. 37. 22, 24. cap. 37. p. 462. If it be no Hæresie to say, the Ten Tribes are the* Sheep: *Why should it be accounted Hæresie to say,* America *is the distinct* Fold *there implied? For Christ doth not affirm that there shall be one* Fold; *but that there shall be ONE FLOCK, ONE SHEPHERD!*

H. R. Trevor-Roper *writes frequently on historical subjects for* HORIZON. *His most recent article was "The Persecution of Witches" in the issue of November, 1959.*

WHAT GOOD IS TELEVISION

CONTINUED FROM PAGE 5

But I could not miss the "visual essay" and expect to make up my loss.

The combination of values was not merely shrewd or ingenious. It was native to the instrument for which it was designed. The essay was possible because of the intimacy and ease of a situation involving a few listeners in the relative quiet of their homes: good essays are usually "casual." And the scale of illustration, the freedom of the essayist to summon up a veritable universe of dancers (or to bring the Philharmonic in for the afternoon), was possible because millions of such intimate situations had been created across the country, quite enough to encourage a sponsor to pay for all the prancing examples. The special contradiction that gives television its hitherto unheard-of character—a mass experience that is also a solitary experience—had here fashioned a dress to fit, had made a gesture completely in accordance with its own most complex and private nature. It had expressed itself.

Such self-expression and assertion of identity have not been confined to a handful of programs devised by Leonard Bernstein and Agnes de Mille, Edward R. Murrow or *Camera Three*. These things have appeared, with quite another set of habits, in such an experiment as the *Project 20* recapitulation, in still photographs, of the life of Abraham Lincoln. In *Meet Mr. Lincoln* (produced in February, 1959, and repeated this year) something uniquely suited to a curious new medium once again caught most of us by surprise. What we were looking at was neither a motion picture nor a parlor scrapbook. One of the two or three basic laws of motion pictures is that the separate images must move, but these images did not move. They were, quite simply, the forever frozen snapshots made by Matthew Brady and the caricatures made by a dozen political cartoonists of Lincoln's time put back to back. But neither did they constitute a pictorial album which we had to leaf through slowly and so lose the relationship of one image to another. A curious combination of apparently opposed, even contradictory, values took firm imaginative hold: the quiet, close-up, concentrated attention we might give to a treasured picture in the privacy of the study, unexpectedly heightened by the meaningful arrangement and the fluid visual and vocal rhythms made possible by the use of sound film. A camera moved across a perfectly still image; the still image surrendered in shock to another slapped over it; the conjunction of stillness and motion, and of vigorously contending images, was explosive. Two normally separated experiences—the one intimate and reflective, the other busy and constructed—fused to produce a wholly unfamiliar effect, as though a mountain had been seen moving a little. Between the authenticity of the record and the bursting energy with which one portion of it shouldered another for position in the frame, a dead man breathed.

There is also a sense in which television, used in a certain way, has succeeded in making living men breathe. Most of us have seen newspaper photographs of most of the prominent men and women of our time; most of us have heard them speak in newsreels. But as candid as the news photos may have been and as familiar as the newsreels may have made these voices, we have still only known such men and women at a good bit more than arm's length. What television, with its strange public-private atmosphere, suggests at once is the possibility of meeting them at armchair length, of overhearing in our living rooms people who would not normally be found there.

This is not mere opportunistic happenstance; it is a principle derived from the nature of the medium. That it is a valid principle is attested to by the recurring—and each time surprisingly fresh—excitement stirred up when a Mike Wallace, an Edward R. Murrow, a Jack Paar, or a David Susskind makes use of the mixture. The mixture is that of public figure and private tone, of exceptional event and our matter-of-fact view of it. Whether we have attended to Sean O'Casey on his own back steps or to Senator Wayne Morse beating Mr. Wallace at his own game in a smoky studio, we have a habit of describing all such experiences as "conversation," and for very good reason. Although we are not yet free to converse with the person, the person is clearly conversing with us; his deportment is special, and is a distinguishing mark of the form for which it is assumed.

Much as we may enjoy Phil Silvers romping his way through the rogueries of Sergeant Bilko, we are wholly aware that what we are enjoying is, in essence, a filmed short subject and that we should enjoy it quite as much in a movie house—perhaps more, since our laughter would be encouraged and increased by the laughter of many others around us. Television becomes television when the door is opened to Mr. Silvers's apartment, and Mr. Silvers, person to person, turns out not to be Sergeant Bilko. We do not need the movie house or the presence of hundreds of companions for this; indeed, the intimacy would become false and embarrassing in more massive circumstances, as it does whenever Bing Crosby or Greer Garson addresses us directly from a very large screen on behalf of some charity or other.

The visual essay, the rhythmic album, the invitation to drop in on a casual conversation—these are the idiosyncratic traits by which television, as television, has come to be recognized. There is no reason to suppose that there are not more such traits waiting to be uncovered in a form that is still quite young. No one can say what imaginative resources, what quirks of personality, may lie hidden awaiting a test of strength.

The danger is not that television is limited in its own right, but that it may never discover what its own right is,

126

that it will never subject itself to proper tests of strength. When the living is easy, no muscles are flexed, and the living is very easy just now. A television professional can go to sleep counting money as long as millions of feet of old film keep rolling down the Hollywood hillside. If the supply of old film begins to dwindle, he need only buy up the studios that once turned it out and arrange for experienced personnel to begin turning out new film, millions more feet of it. The old film cannot only be turned into new film, as *The Thin Man* and Rin Tin Tin have indicated, it can also be turned into live or taped ghosts. With new costumes *The Bells of St. Mary's* can be made to ring out forever.

Too much from the film vaults? Try the stage. *Winterset* and *Harvey*; and next thing you know, *My Fair Lady* will be on the wing. Plays can also be imitated. "Originals" can be written that not only observe all the laws of tidy stage dramaturgy but observe them so well that they can thereafter be trucked across town to Broadway. Should both Hollywood and Broadway threaten to run dry, there remain the public libraries: not all of Jane Austen, not all of Hemingway, not all of Conrad has been triple-spaced down one side of a television manuscript page yet. How soon are we likely to run out of literature?

Most treacherously of all, these things can be done well. Audiences—lazy, temporarily indifferent audiences—may well be grateful for each brilliant instance of mistaken identity. After all, an excellent adaptation of *The Turn of the Screw* saves them the trouble of reading Henry James, at the same time that it saves television the trouble of doing something other than Henry James. There may be quality in the work and a thankful letter in the mail. Television is free to sit under the landslide of borrowed materials because it knows, as it sits, that there is gold in those tumbling hills.

Nevertheless, sitting under a landslide is still one way of committing suicide. Death by drowning in goodies may be a comfortable way of going, but it is death. That patient, sometimes admiring, audience is an erratic and elusive beast, possessed of uncannily right instincts: in some restless, intuitive way it eventually realizes that it is not grappling with the real McCoy and it goes on the prowl to see if it can find out where McCoy lives. While it is never possible to say with finality "These are the *right* things television should do" (because not all of the right things have been discovered yet), it is perfectly possible to say "These are the wrong things" and to forecast the time of the prowl.

The rule of thumb is negative but simple: whenever a form spends its time doing what another medium can do as well, or better, it is headed straight and swift for the boneyard. Boredom is coming; the surrender of audiences to media with more distinctive personalities is coming; failure at the heart, followed by failure at the bank, is coming.

All of these notices from the sheriff have been handed to rival media at one time or another and in one degree or another. We are accustomed to saying, nowadays, that motion pictures lost their stranglehold on the mass imagination because television came along and was both handier and free. Did you know that at the very time the movies were presumably capitulating to television in the large cities, motion-picture attendance fell off to precisely the same degree in mountainous areas where there was no television? Competition always makes inroads, but the size of the dent depends largely upon the vulnerability of the form that is attacked. The dent in this instance was enormous: in a three-year period Chicago alone lost two hundred movie houses. The catastrophe reached such proportions, I am firmly convinced, because the art of film was at that moment at its most vulnerable. It had spent eight to twelve years steadily refining processes calculated to corrupt its own best nature.

Example. When films first broke on the world, let's say with the full-length, full-scale achievement of D. W. Griffith, *The Birth of a Nation*, one of its most persuasive and hitherto unexperienced powers lay in the absolute reality of the moving image. The camera is a scientific instrument, not a paintbrush: its special virtues are accuracy and actuality. Thus, when Griffith organized a pan-shot which began with a mother and child huddled in terror on a mountain and then moved slowly to a raging battle on the plain beneath, we were left breathless by a juxtaposition in scale—from the individual to the group, from the passive to the active—that was, quite literally, taking place before our eyes. Our belief in the medium had begun with actual railroad trains roaring down actual tracks right at us, with actual ocean waves breaking somewhere near our feet. Griffith moved from simple documentation to high imagination, from fact to fiction, from present to past; and he took us with him because he used his camera as a faithful recorder of something that was really and truly going on: he did not abandon his camera's ability to state visual facts.

It is quite a long time since we have had such a pan-shot, not because Griffith had no competent successors but because his latter-day successors have forgotten first principles. The same shot today would begin with a reasonably real close-up of mother and child, perhaps compromised slightly by the color camera, which is not so accurate about color as black-and-white cameras were accurate about lines and shapes. It would then begin its pan toward the valley. As the valley began to come into view, something else would come into view: a thin, fuzzy, indeterminate line indicating that we were now being confronted with a "process" shot. We would realize, as we now always do, that we were looking not at one picture but at two, or rather at two halves of a picture: one shot in a studio, no doubt, and the other shot on location, both to be matched up—almost—later on. The foreground would have a clear texture, the background a grainy one. Now the imaginative ground plan, the meaning of the shot, remains; what has been stripped from it is its power to delight as a record of an actual event, as an actual contrast, as an actual movement through space. We are not looking at something somebody filmed; we are looking at something somebody faked. Hollywood has removed precisely what thrilled audiences in the first instance; and Hollywood is surprised to discover that audiences are disenchanted.

The use of the easy way, the substitute way, the unnatural way inevitably and instinctively leads to a loss of faith.

The other substitutes for the sense of actuality in which a rich and fat Hollywood indulged itself are well known to us: the dubbing of voices, for instance. It was one thing to hear Maurice Chevalier animate a song he was singing; it is quite another to sit through a *Carmen Jones* in which Harry Belafonte and Dorothy Dandridge go through the motions but do not sing. The image before us is fragmentized, our minds turn this way and that. The picture before us is anything but a true one—it is not even all of a piece.

CinemaScope—followed by other large-screen devices— came into being not as a result of some director's inspiration for bettering the medium but as a result of a box-office decline presumably brought about by television. In one sense it offered an intelligent response to the unhappy situation: it tried to be what television could not be—vast—and so to reassert its identity. Unfortunately, for a time at least, it neglected to weigh in the balance those aspects of its identity it might lose in the adaptation to a new panoramic size. It was, for one thing, brushing perilously close to the shape, and the acting techniques, of the legitimate theater's present proscenium arch. There was the terrible danger that the elongated rectangular image would look like a stage set: that the director would begin to manage his actors as though they were in a stage set, asking them to slog across the entire frame at a realistic rate, and that both of these duplicated effects would be imposed without a corresponding gain, without benefit of the theater's very special virtue—dimensional actors emphatically present.

Much more alarming, however, was the loss (and it is still not made up) of what the film theorists call montage: the rapid-fire, vividly subjective placing and cutting of camera angles. The wild rhythms that once hurtled us from close-up to long shot, from terrified eyes to advancing truck to neighbor's glance to bird's-eye view, and all in a blinding rush, were much too wild and much too rhythmic to be applied to CinemaScope's enormous canvas. We should grow dizzy trying to grasp so expansive an image at so rapid a rate.

Another of the most characteristic tools of the motion-picture maker was being blunted. Because the camera can be anywhere, it is obliged to be everywhere, and in the twinkling of an eye. But the camera eye was no longer twinkling: it was staring long and hard, and from right to left, and the experience was far less lively.

The earliest talking films are intolerable today because they were not films but photographed stage plays. The earliest CinemaScope films, beginning with *The Robe*, are nearly as intolerable because they seem to be high school pageants shot by a home-movie maker who could find no more than three possible positions in the auditorium. The more creative film directors are now working furiously to overcome the uncharacteristic stasis imposed by an unwieldy frame. In *The Bridge on the River Kwai*, for instance, David Lean tackled the problem brilliantly in two ways: he made swift montages of his long shots as frequently as he dared; and he explored such untapped advantages as the boxcar shape might possess, making great capital of picking out a distant, tiny figure in the upper right corner and bringing him across the frame and toward us at the same time. The struggle, at this moment, is to see whether the identity of film can be preserved in a size and shape that tend to deny that identity; it is still too early to say whether or not the struggle will prove successful.

Neither has the legitimate theater escaped the penalties of failing to answer to its name. Its most notorious lapse in our time took the form of a scenic binge, a drunken holiday on heavy-laden turntables, during which it tried very hard to do everything Hollywood could do, worse. An awakening is upon us: even as we watch, the theater is urgently embroiled in an effort to rid itself of its schizophrenic tendencies and to reassert those personality quirks that it alone possesses. Contact between living actor and living audience is being stressed; reliance upon words, rather than pictures, is increasing. The stage is learning to say "Never mind everybody else, What am I?" and it may catch more flies with character than it ever did with stolen honey. It has, of course, been through all of this before. When we read that a certain ancient Roman version of the Agamemnon story presented its audience with a Clytemnestra preceded by six hundred mules, we can be fairly certain that drama was being diminished donkey by donkey, and that the theater engaged in such practices might just as well have given up the ghost, then and there, to its rivals the gladiators. Embracing a rival is like running on a sword.

A form in false face, in borrowed finery, is a form that will one day fail to be recognized. The quality of the finery will not save the day, neither will the skill with which the mask is worn. Behind the trappings lies a nonentity, a wax dummy. We shall pass it in the shopwindow without a second glance; in our homes it will be something to stuff in our closets.

A form can have the impulse of life and then be aborted just as whole cultures have stirred and then, through a failure of ego that became a failure of energy, subsided without leaving any firm signature in the sand. It will be interesting to see whether television becomes a mere convenience to be replaced by more convenient conveniences or whether it makes a stubborn little place for itself in the memory of man.

Walter Kerr, drama critic of the New York Herald Tribune, *is known also as playwright and author of television scripts.*

THE
COMIC HISTORY OF ENGLAND

COLORED ETCHINGS BY JOHN LEECH

The Victorians were greedy about history. When they weren't making it, they were reading it—endlessly and, for the authors, profitably. Did Macaulay's thunderous prose and majestic perspectives occasionally pall? Then readers happily dropped his *History of England* for *The Comic History of England*. This remorselessly jocose work, first published in 1847, was written by a lawyer with the memorable name of Gilbert Abbott à Beckett (his family claimed direct descent from the father of Saint Thomas à Becket) and illustrated by John Leech. Both men were members of the original staff of *Punch*. Today à Beckett's text is pretty hard to take ("Caesar, who might have been so called from his readiness to seize upon everything . . ."), but Leech's hand-colored etchings retain their original charm and humor. In this portfolio, HORIZON presents his versions of fourteen high spots of English history.

Landing of Julius Cæsar.

William inspecting the Volunteers previous to the Invasion of England.

Terrific combat between Richard Cœur de Lion and Saladin.

King John Signing Magna Charta.

Coronation of Henry the Fourth (from the best Authorities).

Embarkation of King Henry the Fifth at Southampton. A.D. 1415.

Marriage of Henry the Sixth and Margaret of Anjou.

Henry VIII.th meeting Francis I.st

Henry VIII Monk Hunting.

Queen Elizabeth and Sir Walter Raleigh.